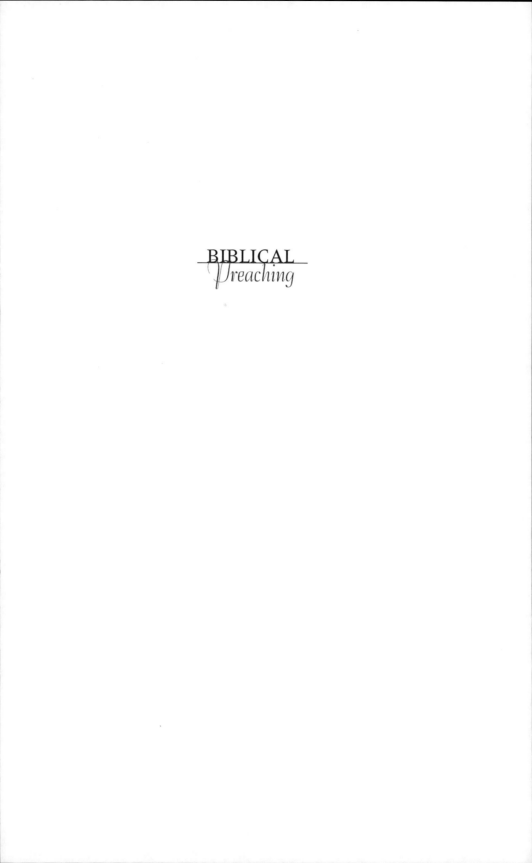

BIBLICAL
Preaching

BIBLICAL
Preaching

*The Development and Delivery
of Expository Messages*

Second Edition

Haddon W. Robinson

Baker Academic
Grand Rapids, Michigan

© 1980, 2001 by Haddon W. Robinson

Published by Baker Academic
a division of Baker Publishing Group
P.O. Box 6287, Grand Rapids, MI 49516–6287
www.bakeracademic.com

Sixth printing, June 2005

Printed in the United States of America

Library of Congress Cataloging-in-Publication Data
Robinson, Haddon W.
    Biblical preaching : the development and delivery of expository messages /
Haddon W. Robinson—2nd ed.
        p. cm.
    Includes bibliographical references and index.
    ISBN 0-8010-2262-2 (cloth)
        1. Preaching. 2. Bible—Homiletical use. I. Title
    BV4211.3 .R59 2001
    251—dc21   00-048606

To the men and women
who keep a sacred appointment
on Sunday morning.
Bewildered by seductive voices,
nursing wounds life has inflicted upon them,
anxious about matters that do not matter.
Yet they come to listen for a clear word from God
that speaks to their condition.

And to those who minister to them now
and those who will do so in the future.

CONTENTS

PREFACE TO THE

Second Edition

Twenty years have passed since I first wrote *Biblical Preaching*. Twenty years. In terms of a person's life, that's a long time. In the words of Charles Dickens, they have been the best of times and the worst of times. The painful times put a new note in my preaching—a sympathy with sinners and a cherishing of God's grace. Unfortunately I have no way to put that into this book.

In the twenty years that have passed, I have been delighted and surprised by those who have purchased *Biblical Preaching*. I have persuaded myself that some have even read it. Students in my classes at Denver Seminary and Gordon-Conwell Theological Seminary have had to read it as an assignment. As a group they have spoken well of it. Students at other schools have also used it as a text. On occasion they have been kind enough to drop me a note of appreciation or have found me at a conference to tell me that the book gave them some guidance for their preaching.

Seasoned veterans who studied preaching back in the dark ages have spoken well of it and have used it for a refresher course. I am gratified by the response.

Then why a second edition? Well, I have changed. I am older now and perhaps a bit wiser. I see some matters more clearly now than I did two decades ago. I haven't changed my basic procedure: sermons must deal with ideas or they deal with nothing. As I have reread these pages, however, I have realized I possess an uncanny ability to make clear things dim. Some sections of the book, therefore, have been largely rewritten to take another run at what I wanted to say.

Feedback from students also prodded me to change some of the exercises at the conclusion of the first chapters. Some of the original material was too complicated and abstract, and it frustrated readers more than it helped them. I've attempted to do better.

I've also changed my language to reflect my theology. God doesn't distribute his gifts by gender. Both women and men have the ability and responsibility to communicate God's Word. I have always believed that, but the language in my first book reflected a distinct male bias. To those women who have used my book in spite of that, I express my thanks for their grace. In this revision I hope I have demonstrated the fruits of my repentance.

In the last twenty years, the culture has changed. Television and the computer have influenced the ways we learn and think. Narrative preaching has come into vogue and reflects the reality that listeners in a television culture think with pictures in their heads. I have spent a bit more time talking about narrative preaching this time around. Inductive sermons also reflect the influence of a storied culture. Although I wrote about induction twenty years ago, I have given it more emphasis in the revision.

Many other authors have written about preaching in the last twenty years. I have not only expanded the bibliography at the conclusion of the book to bring it up to date, but at the end of several chapters I have suggested books for further study.

In the first preface I mentioned an honor roll of people who influenced me in a special way. All of them are to be thanked again. I would like to add my friend Scott Gibson to the list. He is a valued associate who has left a thumbprint on my life. Sid Buzzell, Terry Mattingly, and Don Sunukjian have taught by my side in the Doctor of Ministry track in preaching at Gordon-Conwell. As they have taught the participants in the program, they have taught me a great deal.

I owe an unpayable debt to Alice Mathews, who has a noble heart and a splendid mind. She not only gave me valuable suggestions, but out of her busy schedule of writing and lecturing, she has invested hours on the manuscript. I know the value of her time. Socrates once asked a simple old man what he was most thankful for. The old fellow answered, "That being such as I am, I have had the friends I have had." That is how I feel.

Finally, once again I give thanks to my wife, Bonnie. In our fifty years together, her warmth has not cooled nor her beauty dimmed. She is a remarkable woman. I have never gotten over the fact that she chose to marry me.

PREFACE TO THE
First Edition

When reading a book I have sometimes thought of the preface as material to be skipped. It resembled hymns in a badly planned service. The author inserted it as a buffer before he got down to the business of his book.

As an author, however, I regard the preface as an absolute necessity. I write this volume with no little hesitancy, and the preface permits me to file a needed disclaimer. The literature of homiletics features the names of brilliant preachers and superior teachers. One should think twice—and twice again—before nominating himself to that company.

A reader might understandably assume that anyone writing about preaching must consider himself a master of the discipline. Not so! I have preached my share of forgettable sermons. I know the agony of preparing a message and then having preached it, feeling that I knew naked nothing about the preaching art.

If I can claim any qualification, it is this: I am a good listener. During two decades in the classroom I have evaluated nearly six thousand student sermons. My friends marvel that after listening to hundreds of fledgling preachers stumble through their first sermons, I am not an atheist. Yet while listening I have learned what goes into an effective sermon, and I think I have discovered what to do and what to avoid. As a teacher of preachers, I'm a bit like Leo Durocher. While playing baseball his batting average was not much bigger than his shirt size, but as a manager he coached a number of successful teams.

Many of my students have gone on to be effective communicators of the Word of God, and they assure me that in some small way I have had an influence on their ministries. They and I both know that rules of homiletics do not in themselves produce effective preachers. The student must carry to the task some gift and even more, an unquenchable desire to bring a passage of Scripture into contact with life. Richard Baxter once commented that he never knew a man worth anything in his ministry who lacked a desire bordering on unhappiness to see the fruit of his labor. Principles and passion must be united before much of significance occurs in the pulpit. In this book, therefore, I pass on a method to those learning to preach or to experienced people who want to brush up on the basics. Hopefully I have expressed myself clearly enough that laymen—men and women—who teach the Scriptures will benefit. Yet to this material a reader brings himself—his life, insights, maturity, imagination, and dedication. Like hydrogen and oxygen producing water, desire and instruction together make effective communicators of God's truth.

When I started teaching, I did not intend to write. All I wanted to do was find enough usable advice to provide my students a way to proceed as they prepared to preach. In desperation for something sensible to say, I read widely. Of my debt to others I can hardly say enough. For example, H. Grady Davis made a special contribution. As I was attempting to find my way, his book found me. While he might want to disown any connection with this volume, his *Design for Preaching* proved yeast for my thinking. I have drawn from myriad other sources as well—some now forgotten, but not deliberately. To those unacknowledged contributors, I plead the experience of Homer as reported by Rudyard Kipling:

> When 'Omer smote 'is bloomin' lyre,
>   He'd 'eard men sing by land an' sea;
> An' what the thought 'e might require,
>   'E went an' took—the same as me!
>
> The market-girls an' fishermen,
>   The shepherds an' the sailors, too,
> They 'eard old songs turn up again,
>   But kep' it quiet—same as you!
>
> They knew 'e stole; 'e knew they knowed.
>   They didn't tell, nor make a fuss,
> But winked at 'Omer down the road,
>   An' 'e winked back—the same as us![1]

I acknowledge my debt to scores of others. To those students who raised the questions that I was driven to answer and who told me in gentle ways when I simply did not make myself clear, I owe much more than thanks. My former colleagues at Dallas Theological Seminary contributed far more than they realize. Duane Litfin, John Reed, Mike Cocoris, Elliott Johnson, Harold Hoehner, and Zane Hodges, among others, are men who love God with their minds—and who are not hesitant to speak them. Bruce Waltke of Regent College contributed enormously to my life over twenty years and provided a model of scholarship related to life. Since all of these and others influenced me deeply, it is only fair that for weaknesses in this volume they should shoulder a large share of the blame!

Nancy Hardin deserves special mention. Not only did she prepare and type the manuscript, but like a vigilant sentry she guarded my time so that I could find opportunities to write.

---

1. *Rudyard Kipling's Verse: 1885–1926* (Garden City, N.Y.: Doubleday, Page, 1927), p. 403.

And my wife, Bonnie! How much I owe her! Only she knows as she reads these words how much she has done for me. Only I can know the profound influence she has had on my life.

Now that the preface is written, we can be on to the task. Anyone sensitive to the Scriptures knows the awe of the ministry. Matthew Simpson in his *Lectures on Preaching* put the preacher in his place: "His throne is the pulpit; he stands in Christ's stead; his message is the word of God; around him are immortal souls; the Savior, unseen, is beside him; the Holy Spirit broods over the congregation; angels gaze upon the scene, and heaven and hell await the issue. What associations, and what vast responsibility!"[2]

2. (New York: Phillips & Hunt, 1879), p. 166.

one

THE CASE FOR
Expository Preaching

This is a book about expository preaching, but it may have been written for a depressed market. Not everyone agrees that expository preaching—or any sort of preaching, for that matter—is an urgent need of the church. The word is out in some circles that preaching should be abandoned. The moving finger has passed it by and now points to other methods and ministries that are more "effective" and in tune with the times.

THE DEVALUATION OF PREACHING

To explain why preaching receives these low grades would take us into every area of our common life. Because preachers are no longer regarded as the intellectual or even the spiritual leaders in their communities, their image has changed. Ask people in the pews to describe a minister, and their description may not be flattering. According to Kyle Haselden, the pastor comes across as a "bland composite" of the congregation's "congenial, ever helpful, ever ready to help boy scout; as the darling of the old ladies and as sufficiently reserved with the young ones; as the father image for the young people and a companion to lonely men; as the affable glad-hander at teas and civic club luncheons."[1] If that description pictures reality at all, preachers may be liked, but they will certainly not be respected.

In addition, preaching takes place in an over-communicated society. Mass media bombard us with a hundred thousand "messages" a day. Television and radio feature pitchmen delivering a "word from the sponsor" with all the sincerity of an evangelist. Within that context the preacher may sound like another huckster who, in John Ruskin's words, "plays stage tricks with the doctrines of life and death."

More important, perhaps, is that some ministers in the pulpit feel robbed of an authoritative message. Much modern theology offers them little more than holy hunches, and they suspect that the sophisticates in the pew place more faith in science texts than in preaching texts. For some preachers, therefore, fads in communication become more alluring than the message. Multimedia presentations, videos, sharing sessions, blinking lights, and up-to-date music may be symptoms of either health or disease. Undoubtedly, modern techniques can enhance communication, but on the other hand, they can substitute for the message. The startling and unusual may mask a vacuum.

Social action appeals more to a segment of the church than talking or listening. What good are words of faith, they ask, when society demands works of faith? Some people with this mind-set judge that the apostles had things turned around when they decided, "It is not right that we should forsake the Word of God to serve tables" (Acts 6:2 ASV). In a day of activism, it is more relevant

---

1. Kyle Haselden, *The Urgency of Preaching* (New York: Harper and Row, 1963), pp. 88–89. Note that full bibliographical information is not supplied in the footnotes for books included in the bibliography. Nor is bibliographical information that is given in the text repeated in the footnotes.

to declare instead, "It is not right that we should forsake the service of tables to preach the Word of God."

THE CASE FOR PREACHING

In spite of the "bad-mouthing" of preaching and preachers, no one who takes the Bible seriously should count preaching out. To the New Testament writers, preaching stands as the event through which God works. Peter, for example, reminded his readers that they had "been born anew, not of perishable seed but of imperishable, through the living and abiding word of God" (1 Peter 1:23 RSV). How had this word come to affect their lives? "That word," Peter explained, "is the good news which was preached to you" (1:25). Through preaching God had redeemed them.

Paul was a writer. From his pen we have most of the inspired letters of the New Testament, and heading the list of his letters is the one to the Romans. Measured by its impact on history, few documents compare with it. Yet when Paul wrote this letter to the congregation in Rome, he confessed, "I long to see you, that I may impart to you some spiritual gift to strengthen you, that is, that we may be mutually encouraged by each other's faith, both yours and mine" (Rom. 1:11–12 RSV). Paul realized that some ministries simply cannot take place apart from face-to-face contact. Even the reading of an inspired letter will not substitute. "I am eager to preach the gospel to you . . . who are in Rome" (1:15 RSV). A power comes through the preached word that even the written word cannot replace.

Moreover, Paul recounted the spiritual history of the Thessalonians who had "turned to God from idols, to serve a living and true God, and to wait for his Son from heaven" (1 Thess. 1:9–10 RSV). That about-face occurred, explained the apostle, because "when you received the word of God which you heard from us, you accepted it not as the word of men but as what it actually is, the word of God, which is at work in you believers" (2:13 RSV). Preaching in Paul's mind did not consist of someone discussing religion. Instead, God Himself spoke through the personality and message of a preacher to confront men and women and bring them to Himself.

All of this explains why Paul encouraged his young associate Timothy to "preach the Word" (2 Tim. 4:2). Preach means "to cry out, herald, or exhort." Preachers should pour out the message with passion and fervor in order to stir souls. Not all passionate pleading from a pulpit, however, possesses divine authority. When preachers speak as heralds, they must cry out "the Word." Anything less cannot legitimately pass for Christian preaching.

THE NEED FOR EXPOSITORY PREACHING

Those in the pulpit face the pressing temptation to deliver some message other than that of the Scriptures—a political system (either right-wing or left-wing), a theory of economics, a new religious philosophy, old religious slogans, or a trend in psychology. Ministers can proclaim anything in a stained-glass voice at 11:30 on Sunday morning following the singing of hymns. Yet when they fail to preach the Scriptures, they abandon their authority. No longer do they confront their hearers with a word from God. That is why most modern preaching evokes little more than a wide yawn. God is not in it.

God speaks through the Bible. It is the major tool of communication by which He addresses individuals today. Biblical preaching, therefore, must not be equated with "the old, old story of Jesus and His love" as though it were retelling history about better times when God was alive and well. Nor is preaching merely a rehash of ideas about God—orthodox, but removed from life. Through the preaching of the Scriptures, God encounters men and women to bring them to salvation (2 Tim. 3:15) and to richness and ripeness of Christian character (vv. 16–17). Something fills us with awe when God confronts individuals through preaching and seizes them by the soul.

The type of preaching that best carries the force of divine authority is expository preaching. It would be fatuous, however, to assume that everyone agrees with that statement. A poll of churchgoers who have squirmed for hours under "expository" preaching that is dry as corn flakes without milk could not be expected to agree. While most preachers tip their hats to expository preaching, their practice gives them away. Because they seldom do it, they too vote no.

Admittedly, expository preaching has suffered severely in the pulpits of those claiming to be its friends. Yet not all expository preaching necessarily qualifies as either *expository* or *preaching*. Regrettably the Bureau of Weights and Measures does not have a standard expository sermon encased in glass against which to compare other messages. Ministers may paste the label *expository* on whatever sermon they please, and no consumer advocate will correct them. Yet, in spite of damage done by admirers, genuine expository preaching has behind it the power of the living God.

What, then, is the real thing? What constitutes expository preaching? How does it compare or contrast with other kinds of preaching?

THE DEFINITION OF EXPOSITORY PREACHING

Attempting a definition becomes sticky business because what we define we sometimes destroy. The small boy who dissected a frog to find out what made it jump learned something about the parts in the process, but he killed the frog. Preaching is a living interaction involving God, the preacher, and the congregation, and no definition can pretend to capture that dynamic. But for the sake of clarity we must attempt a working definition anyway.

Expository preaching is the communication of a biblical concept, derived from and transmitted through a historical, grammatical, and literary study of a passage in its context, which the Holy Spirit first applies to the personality and experience of the preacher, then through the preacher, applies to the hearers.

The Passage Governs the Sermon

What particulars of this elaborate and somewhat dry definition should we highlight? First, and above all, the thought of the biblical writer determines the substance of an expository ser-

mon. In many sermons the biblical passage read to the congregation resembles the national anthem played at a baseball game—
it gets things started but is not heard again during the afternoon.
In expository preaching, as R. H. Montgomery describes it, "the
preacher undertakes the presentation of particular books [of the
Bible] as some men would undertake the latest best seller. The
preacher seeks to bring the message of definite units of God's
Word to his people."

Expository preaching at its core is more a philosophy than a
method. Whether or not we can be called expositors starts with
our purpose and with our honest answer to the question: "Do
you, as a preacher, endeavor to bend your thought to the Scriptures, or do you use the Scriptures to support your thought?"
This is not the same question as, "Is what you are preaching orthodox or evangelical?" Nor is it the same as, "Do you hold a high
view of the Bible or believe it to be the infallible Word of God?"
As important as these questions may appear in other circumstances, a passing grade in systematic theology does not qualify
an individual as an expositor of the Bible. Theology may protect
us from evils lurking in atomistic, nearsighted interpretations,
but at the same time it may blindfold us from seeing the text. In
approaching a passage, we must be willing to reexamine our doc-
trinal convictions and to reject the judgments of our most respected teachers. We must make a U-turn in our own previous
understandings of the Bible should these conflict with the concepts of the biblical writer.

Adopting this attitude toward Scripture demands both simplicity and sophistication. On the one hand, expositors approach
their Bible with a childlike desire to hear the story. They do not
come to argue, to prove a point, or even to find a sermon. They
read to understand and to experience what they understand. At
the same time, they know they live not as children but as adults
locked into presuppositions and worldviews that make understanding difficult. The Bible is not a child's storybook; rather it is
great literature that requires thoughtful response. All its dia-
monds do not lie exposed on the surface. Its richness is mined
only through hard intellectual and spiritual spadework.

The Expositor Communicates a Concept

The definition of expository preaching also emphasizes that an expositor communicates a concept. Some conservative preachers have been led astray by their doctrine of inspiration and by a poor understanding of how language works. Orthodox theologians insist that the Holy Spirit protects the individual words of the original text. Words are the stuff from which ideas are made, they argue, and unless the words are inspired, the ideas cannot be guarded from error.

While an orthodox doctrine of inspiration may be a necessary plank in the evangelical platform on biblical authority, this sometimes gets in the way of expository preaching. Although we examine words in the text and sometimes deal with particular words in the sermon, words and phrases should never become ends in themselves. Words are stupid things until linked with other words to convey meaning.

In our approach to the Bible, therefore, we are primarily concerned not with what individual words mean, but with what the biblical writers mean through their use of words. Putting this another way, we do not understand the concepts of a passage merely by analyzing its separate words. A word-by-word grammatical analysis can be as pointless and boring as reading a dictionary. If we desire to understand the Bible in order to communicate its message, we must grapple with it on the level of ideas.

Francis A. Schaeffer, in his book *True Spirituality*, argues that the great battles take place in the realm of thought:

> Ideas are the stock of the thought-world, and from the ideas burst forth all the external things—painting, music, buildings, the love and the hating of men in practice, and equally the results of loving God or rebellion against God in the external world. . . . The preaching of the gospel is ideas, flaming ideas brought to men, as God has revealed them to us in Scripture. It is not a contentless experience internally received, but it is contentful ideas internally acted upon that make the difference. So when we state our doctrines, they must be ideas and not just phrases. We cannot use doctrines as though they were mechanical pieces to a puzzle. True doctrine is an idea revealed by God in the Bible and an idea that

fits properly into the external world as it is, and as God made it, and to man as he is as God made him, and can be fed back through man's body into his thought-world and there acted upon. The battle for man is centrally in the world of thought.[2]

If we are ever to get sermons, therefore, we must get them first as ideas.

The Concept Comes from the Text

This emphasis on ideas as the substance of expository preaching does not in any way deny the importance of vocabulary or grammar. The definition goes on to explain that in the expository sermon the idea is derived from and transmitted through a historical, grammatical, and literary study of a passage in its context. This deals first with how expositors come to their message and, second, with how they communicate it. Both involve the examination of grammar, history, and literary forms. In their study expositors search for the objective meaning of a passage through their understanding of the language, backgrounds, and setting of the text. Then in the pulpit they present enough of their study to the congregation so that their listeners may check the interpretation for themselves.

Ultimately the authority behind expository preaching resides not in the preacher but in the biblical text. For that reason expositors deal largely with an explanation of Scripture, so that they focus the listener's attention on the Bible. Expositors may be respected for their exegetical abilities and their diligent preparation, but these qualities do not transform any of them into a Protestant pope who speaks *ex cathedra*. Listeners also have a responsibility to match the sermon to the biblical text. As Henry David Thoreau wrote, "It takes two to speak the truth—one to speak, and another to hear." No truth worth knowing will be acquired without a tussle, so if a congregation is to grow, it must share the struggle. "To have great poets, there must be great audiences," Walt Whitman confessed. Effective expository preaching requires listeners with ears to hear. Since the souls of listeners depend upon it, we

---

2. Francis A. Schaeffer, *True Spirituality* (Wheaton: Tyndale, 1971), pp. 121–22.

must offer our hearers sufficient information so that they can decide for themselves if what they are hearing is indeed what the Bible says.

If the listeners in the pew must work to understand the preacher, the preacher must labor to understand the writers of the Bible. Communication means "a meeting of meanings," and for communication to occur across a sanctuary or across the centuries, those involved must share things in common—a language, a culture, a worldview, communication forms. We try to pull up our chairs to where the biblical authors sat. We attempt to work our way back into the world of the Scriptures to understand the original message. Though we may not master the languages, history, and literary forms of the biblical writers, we should appreciate the contribution of each of these disciplines. We should also become aware of the wide assortment of interpretive aids available to us for use in our study.[3] As much as possible, expositors seek a firsthand acquaintance with the biblical writers and their ideas in context.

The Concept Is Applied to the Expositor

Our definition of expository preaching goes on to say that the truth must be applied to the personality and experience of the preacher. This places God's dealing with the preacher at the center of the process. As much as we might wish it otherwise, we cannot be separated from the message. Who has not heard some devout brother or sister pray in anticipation of a sermon, "Hide our pastor behind the cross so that we may see not him but Jesus only"? We commend the spirit of such a prayer. Men and women must get past the preacher to the Savior. (Or perhaps the Savior must get past the preacher to the people!)

Yet no place exists where a preacher may hide. Even a large pulpit cannot conceal us from view. Phillips Brooks was on to something when he described preaching as "truth poured through personality."[4] We affect our message. We may be

---

3. Some of these aids will be discussed in chapter 3.
4. Phillips Brooks, *Lectures on Preaching* (New York: Dutton, 1877), p. 8.

mouthing a scriptural idea, yet we can remain as impersonal as a
telephone recording, as superficial as a radio commercial, or as
manipulative as a con man. The audience does not hear a sermon, they hear a person—they hear you.

Bishop William A. Quayle had this in mind when he rejected
standard definitions of homiletics. "Preaching is the art of making a sermon and delivering it?" he asked. "Why, no, that is not
preaching. Preaching is the art of making a preacher and delivering that!" A commitment to expository preaching should develop the preacher into a mature Christian. As we study our Bible, the Holy Spirit studies us. As we prepare expository sermons,
God prepares us. As P. T. Forsyth said, "The Bible is the supreme
preacher to the preacher."[5]

Distinctions made between "studying the Bible to get a sermon
and studying the Bible to feed your own soul" are misleading and
even false. A scholar may examine the Bible as Hebrew poetry or
as a record of the births and reigns of long-dead kings and yet not
be confronted by its truth. Yet no such detachment can exist for
one who opens the Bible as the Word of God. Before we proclaim
the message of the Bible to others, we should live with that message ourselves.

Regrettably, many preachers fail as Christians before they fail
as preachers because they do not think biblically. A significant
number of ministers, many of whom profess high regard for the
Scriptures, prepare their sermons without consulting the Bible at
all. While the sacred text serves as an appetizer to get a sermon
underway or as a garnish to decorate the message, the main
course consists of the preacher's own thought or someone else's
thought warmed up for the occasion.

Even in what is billed as "expository preaching" individual
verses can become launching pads for the preacher's own opinions. One common recipe found in homiletical cookbooks reads
something like this: "Take several theological or moral plati-
tudes, mix with equal parts of 'dedication,' 'evangelism,' or
'stewardship,' add several 'kingdoms' or 'the Bible says,' stir in a

---

5. P. T. Forsyth, *Positive Preaching and the Modern Mind* (Grand Rapids: Eerdmans,
1964), p. 11.

selection of stories, add 'salvation' to taste. Serve hot on a bed of Scripture verses." Such sermons not only leave a congregation undernourished, but they also starve the preachers. They do not grow because the Holy Spirit has nothing to feed them. William Barclay diagnosed the cause of spiritual malnutrition in a minister's life when he pointed out that if our minds grow slack and lazy and flabby, the Holy Spirit cannot speak to us. "True preaching comes when the loving heart and the disciplined mind are laid at the disposal of the Holy Spirit."[6] Ultimately God is more interested in developing messengers than messages, and because the Holy Spirit confronts us primarily through the Bible, we must learn to listen to God before speaking for God.

The Concept Is Applied to the Hearers

Not only does the Holy Spirit apply His truth to the personality and experience of the preacher, but according to our definition of expository preaching, He then applies that truth through the preacher to the hearers. Expositors think in three areas. First, as exegetes, we struggle with the meanings of the biblical writer. Then, as people of God, we wrestle with how God wants to change us. Finally, as preachers, we ponder what God wants to say to the congregation through us.

Application gives expository preaching purpose. As shepherds, we relate to the hurts, cries, and fears of our flock. Therefore we study the Scriptures, wondering what they can say to people living with grief and guilt, doubt and death. Paul reminded Timothy that the Scriptures were given to be applied. "All scripture is inspired by God," he wrote, "and is useful for teaching the faith and correcting error, for re-setting the direction of a man's life and training him in good living. The scriptures are the comprehensive equipment of the man of God, and fit him fully for all branches of his work" (2 Tim. 3:16–17 PHILLIPS).

Dull expository sermons usually lack effective applications. Boring sermons evoke two major complaints. First, listeners grumble, "It's always the same old thing." The preacher gives all

---

6. William Barclay, *A Spiritual Autobiography* (Grand Rapids: Eerdmans, 1975).

passages the same application, or worse, no application at all. "May the Holy Spirit apply this truth to our lives," incants a minister who does not have a ghost of a guess as to how the biblical content might change people.

A second negative reaction is that the sermon does not relate to the world directly enough to be of practical use: "It's true enough, I guess, but so what? What difference does it make?" After all, if a man or woman decides to live under the mandate of Scripture, such action will normally take place outside the church building. On the outside, people lose jobs, worry about their children, and find crabgrass invading their lawns. Normal people do not lose sleep over the Jebusites, the Canaanites, or the Perizzites, or even about what Abraham, Moses, or Paul has said or done. They lie awake wondering about grocery prices, crop failures, quarrels with a spouse, diagnosis of a malignancy, a frustrating sex life, or the rat race where only rats seem to win. If the sermon does not make much difference in that world, they wonder if it makes any difference at all.

We should forget about speaking to the ages, therefore, and speak to our day. Expository preachers confront people about themselves from the Bible instead of lecturing to them about the Bible's history or archaeology. A congregation does not convene as a jury to convict Judas, Peter, or Solomon, but to judge themselves. We must know the people as well as the message, and to acquire that knowledge, we exegete both the Scripture and the congregation.

After all, when God spoke in the Scriptures, He addressed women and men as they were, where they were. Imagine that Paul's letters to the Corinthians had gotten lost in the mail and instead had been delivered to the Christians at Philippi. The Philippians would have puzzled over the specific problems Paul wrote about because they lived in a situation different from that of their sisters and brothers in Corinth. The letters of the New Testament, like the prophecies of the Old, were addressed to specific assemblies struggling with particular problems. Our expository sermons today will be ineffective unless we realize that our listeners, too, exist at a particular address and have mind-sets unique to them.

Effective application thrusts us into both theology and ethics. Traveling from exegesis to application, we make a hard trip through life-related and sometimes perplexing questions. In addition to grammatical relationships, we also explore personal and psychological relationships. How do the characters in the text relate to one another? How are they related to God? What values lie behind the choices they make? What apparently went on in the minds of those who were involved? These questions are not directed to the "there and then," as though God dealt with men and women only back in the "once upon a time." The same questions can be asked in the "here and now." How do we relate to one another today? How does God confront us about similar issues? In what way does the modern world compare or contrast with the biblical world? Are the questions dealt with in Scripture the questions people ask today? Are they put forth now in the same way or in different forms? These probings become the raw material of ethics and theology. Application tacked on to an expository sermon in an attempt to make it relevant skirts these questions and ignores the maxim of our Protestant forebears: "Doctrines must be preached practically, and duties doctrinally."

Inappropriate application can be as destructive as inept exegesis. When Satan tempted Jesus in the wilderness, he tried to achieve victory through misapplication of Scripture. The tempter whispered Psalm 91 with admirable precision: "He will give his angels charge over you to keep you in all your ways . . . lest you dash your foot against a stone" (vv. 11–12). Then Satan reasoned, "Because you possess this strong promise, why not apply it to a leap from the pinnacle of the temple and demonstrate once and for all that you are the Son of God?" In refuting the devil, Jesus did not debate the grammar of the Hebrew text. Instead He attacked the application of Psalm 91 to temple jumping. Another passage of Scripture better fit that situation: "You shall not tempt the LORD your God" (Deut. 6:16 NRSV).

We must preach to a world addressed by the TV commentator, the newspaper columnist, and the playwright. If we do not, we will have hearers who are orthodox in their heads but heretics in their conduct. Of course in speaking to a secular world we dare not speak a secular word. William Willimon observed that some preachers seem to have bent over backwards to speak to a secular audience and they have fallen in. While biblical ideas must be shaped to human experience, men and women must be called to conform to biblical truth. "Relevant" sermons may become pulpit trifles unless they relate the current situation to the eternal Word of God.

F. B. Meyer understood the awe with which biblical preachers speak to the issues of their age. They are "in a line of great succession. The reformers, the Puritans, the pastors of the Pilgrim fathers were essentially expositors. They did not announce their own particular opinions, which might be a matter of private interpretation or doubtful disposition, but taking their stand on Scripture, drove home their message with irresistible effect with 'Thus saith the Lord.'"

Let's sum this up. We preach expository sermons when

- We have studied a passage in its context, giving attention to its historical, grammatical, and literary setting;
- We have in some way experienced, through the work of the Holy Spirit, the power of our study in our own lives;
- And from this, we shape the sermon so that it communicates the central biblical concept in a way that is meaningful to our hearers.

New Concepts

Expository preaching

Definitions

Expository preaching—the communication of a biblical concept, derived from and transmitted through a historical, grammatical, and literary study of a passage in its context, which the Holy Spirit first applies to the personality and experience of the preacher, then through the preacher, applies to the hearers.

For Further Reading and Reflection

Many writers attempt to define or describe biblical preaching. Some describe the trees and others settle for the forest.

- Richard Mayhue spends a chapter of *Rediscovering Expository Preaching* (Dallas: Word, 1992) grappling with what it is not and then what it is. An expositor, he concludes, "explains the Scripture by laying open the text to public view in order to set forth its meaning, explain what is difficult to understand, and make appropriate application" (p.11).
- Jerry Vines and Jim Shaddix put more emphasis on the listeners in their definition of biblical preaching as "the oral communication of biblical truth by the Holy Spirit through a human personality to a given audience with the intent of enabling a positive response" (*Power in the Pulpit* [Chicago: Moody, 1999], p. 27).
- Bryan Chapell allows for a broader definition when he makes the observation that "any sermon that explores a biblical concept is in the broadest sense 'expository,'" but he cannot leave it there. He adds that "*the technical definition of an expository sermon* [his emphasis] requires that it expound Scripture by deriving from a specific text main points and subpoints that disclose the thought of the author, cover the scope of the

passage, and are applied to the lives of the listeners" (*Christ-Centered Preaching* [Grand Rapids: Baker, 1994], pp. 128–29).

- John Stott, in his book *Between Two Worlds* (Grand Rapids: Eerdmans, 1982), makes the flat statement, "All true preaching is expository preaching." He goes on to say, however, that "expository" refers to content and not to method, and then he describes what it looks like. "In expository preaching the biblical text is neither a conventional introduction to a sermon on a largely different theme, nor a convenient peg on which to hang a ragbag of miscellaneous thoughts, but a master which dictates and controls what is said" (pp. 125–26).

- Fred Craddock, who might not be comfortable with my definition, recognizes that we are wrestling with "a fundamental theological question of authority." He goes to the central issue of what any of us do in the pulpit. "The preacher is obligated, regardless of the sermons the parishioners may like," he says, "to ask and respond to the questions, What authorizes my sermons? If the authorization is by the Scriptures, in what way? How do I prepare so as to enter the pulpit with some confidence that my understanding of biblical preaching has been implemented with honesty and integrity? . . . It is not likely that any preacher will arrive at a satisfactory position that does not involve serious grappling with the text of Scripture" (*Preaching* [Nashville: Abingdon, 1986], p. 100).

On another level, at sometime or other, you will have to respond to the question, "How does the centrality of Jesus Christ affect the way that I handle the biblical texts? If a thoughtful Muslim or a Jew would be satisfied with my interpretation of the Old Testament, could it really be Christian?" Two books that work toward a way of solving this problem are Sidney Greidanus, *Preaching Christ from the Old Testament* (Grand Rapids: Eerdmans, 1999), and Graeme Goldsworthy, *Preaching the Whole Bible as Christian Scripture* (Grand Rapids: Eerdmans, 2000). An older book by Walter Kaiser, *Toward an Exegetical Theology: Biblical Exegesis for Preaching and Teaching* (Grand Rapids: Baker, 1981), approaches the same question from a different angle.

two

WHAT'S THE
Big Idea?

I do not appreciate opera; what is worse, I have several friends who do. Being around them makes me feel as if I exist in a cultural desert, so I have taken several steps to change my condition. On occasion I have actually attended an opera. Like a sinner shamed into attending church, I have made my way to the music hall to let culture have its way in me. On most of these visits, however, I have returned home unresponsive to what the artists have tried to do.

I understand enough about opera, of course, to know that a story is being acted out with the actors singing rather than speaking their parts. Usually, though, the story line stays as vague to me as the Italian lyrics, but opera buffs tell me that the plot is incidental to the performance. Should someone bother to ask my evaluation of the opera, I would comment on the well-constructed sets, the brilliant costumes, or the heftiness of the soprano. I could render no reliable judgment on the interpretation of the music or even the dramatic impact of the performance. When I return from the music hall with a crumpled program and an assortment of random impressions, I actually do not know how to evaluate what has taken place.

When people attend church, they may respond to the preacher like a novice at the opera. They have never been told what a sermon is supposed to do. Commonly many listeners react to the emotional highs. They enjoy the human interest stories, jot down a catchy sentence or two, and judge the sermon a success if the preacher quits on time. Important matters, such as the subject of the sermon, may escape them completely. Years ago Calvin Coolidge returned home from church one Sunday and was asked by his wife what the minister had talked about. Coolidge replied, "Sin." When his wife pressed him as to what the preacher said about sin, Coolidge responded, "I think he was against it."

The truth is that many people in the pew would not score much higher than Coolidge if quizzed about the content of last Sunday's sermon. To them, preachers preach about sin, salvation, prayer, or suffering all together or one at a time in thirty-five minutes. Judging from the uncomprehending way in which listeners talk about a sermon, it is hard to believe that they have listened to a *message*. Instead the responses indicate that they leave with a basketful of fragments but no adequate sense of the whole.

Unfortunately some of us preach as we have listened. Preachers, like their audiences, may conceive of sermons as a collection of points that have little relationship to each other. Here textbooks designed to help speakers may actually hinder them. Discussions of outlining usually emphasize the place of Roman and Arabic numerals along with proper indentation, but these factors (important as they are) may ignore the obvious—an outline is the shape of the sermon idea, and the parts must all be related to the whole. Three or four ideas not related to a more inclusive idea do not make a message; they make three or four sermonettes all preached at one time. Reuel L. Howe listened to hundreds of taped sermons and held discussions with laypeople. He concluded that the people in the pew "complain almost unanimously that sermons often contain too many ideas."[1] That may not be an accurate observation. Sermons seldom fail because they have too many ideas; more often they fail because they deal with too many unrelated ideas.

Fragmentation poses a particular danger for the expository preacher. Some expository sermons offer little more than scattered comments based on words and phrases from a passage, making no attempt to show how the various thoughts fit together as a whole. At the outset the preacher may catch the congregation's mind with some observation about life, or worse, jump into the text with no thought at all about the present. As the sermon goes on, the preacher comments on the words and phrases in the passage with sub-themes and major themes and individual words all given equal emphasis. The conclusion, if there is one, usually substitutes a vague exhortation for relevant application, because no single truth has emerged to apply. When the congregation goes back into the world, it has received no message by which to live because it has not occurred to the preacher to preach one.

A major affirmation of our definition of expository preaching, therefore, maintains that "expository preaching is the communication of a biblical concept." That affirms the obvious. A sermon should be a bullet, not buckshot. Ideally each sermon is the explanation, interpretation, or application of a single dominant idea supported by other ideas, all drawn from one passage or several passages of Scripture.

THE IMPORTANCE OF A SINGLE IDEA

Students of public speaking and preaching have argued for centuries that effective communication demands a single theme. Rhetoricians hold to this so strongly that virtually every textbook

---

1. Reuel L. Howe, *Partners in Preaching: Clergy and Laity in Dialogue,* p. 26.

devotes some space to a treatment of the principle. Terminology may vary—central idea, proposition, theme, thesis statement, main thought—but the concept is the same: an effective speech "centers on one specific thing, a central idea."[2] This thought is so axiomatic to speech communication that some authors, such as Lester Thonssen and A. Craig Baird, take it for granted:

> Little need be said here about the emergence of the central theme. It is assumed that the speech possesses a clearly defined and easily determined thesis or purpose: that this thesis is unencumbered by collateral theses which interfere with the clear perception of the principal one; and that the development is of such a character as to provide for the easy and unmistakable emergence of the thesis through the unfolding of the contents of the speech.[3]

Homileticians join their voices to insist that a sermon, like any good speech, embodies a single, all-encompassing concept. Donald G. Miller, in a chapter devoted to the heart of biblical preaching, insists:

> . . . any single sermon should have just one major idea. The points or subdivisions should be parts of this one grand thought. Just as bites of any particular food are all parts of the whole, cut into sizes that are both palatable and digestible, so the points of a sermon should be smaller sections of the one theme, broken into tinier fragments so that the mind may grasp them and the life assimilate them. . . . We are now ready to state in simplest terms the burden of this chapter. It is this: *Every sermon should have a theme, and that theme should be the theme of the portion of Scripture on which it is based.*[4]

From a different tradition Alan M. Stibbs adds a seconding voice: "The preacher must develop his expository treatment of

---

2. William Norwood Brigance, *Speech: Its Techniques and Disciplines in a Free Society*, p. 35. See also the discussions of the central idea in: Donald C. Bryant and Karl R. Wallace, *Fundamentals of Public Speaking*, 3d ed., pp. 146–48; Milton Dickens, *Speech: Dynamic Communication*, pp. 58, 254–56, 267–71; Alma Johnson Sarett, Lew Sarett, and William Trufant Foster, *Basic Principles of Speech*, p. 215.

3. Lester Thonssen and A. Craig Baird, *Speech Criticism: The Development of Standards for Rhetorical Appraisal*, p. 393.

4. Donald G. Miller, *The Way to Biblical Preaching*, pp. 53–55 (italics in original).

the text in relation to a single dominant theme."[5] H. Grady Davis develops his book, *Design for Preaching*, in support of the thesis that "a well-prepared sermon is the embodiment, the development, the full statement of a significant thought."[6] A classic statement of this concept comes from J. H. Jowett in his Yale lectures on preaching:

> I have a conviction that no sermon is ready for preaching, not ready for writing out, until we can express its theme in a short, pregnant sentence as clear as a crystal. I find the getting of that sentence is the hardest, the most exacting, and the most fruitful labour in my study. To compel oneself to fashion that sentence, to dismiss every word that is vague, ragged, ambiguous, to think oneself through to a form of words which defines the theme with scrupulous exactness—this is surely one of the most vital and essential factors in the making of a sermon: and I do not think any sermon ought to be preached or even written, until that sentence has emerged, clear and lucid as a cloudless moon.[7]

To ignore the principle that a central, unifying idea must be at the heart of an effective sermon is to push aside what experts in both communication theory and preaching have to tell us.[8]

A novice may dismiss the importance of a central idea as the ploy of homiletics professors determined to press young preachers into their mold. It should be noted, therefore, that this basic fact of communication also claims sturdy biblical support. In the Old Testament, the sermons of the prophets are called "the burden of the Lord." These proclamations were not a few "appropriate remarks" delivered because the prophet was expected to say something. Instead the prophet addressed his countrymen because he had something to say. He preached a message, complete and entire, to persuade his hearers to return to God. As a result

---

5. Alan M. Stibbs, *Expounding God's Word: Some Principles and Methods*, p. 40.
6. H. Grady Davis, *Design for Preaching*, p. 20.
7. J. H. Jowett, *The Preacher: His Life and Work*, p. 133.
8. See, for example, Andrew W. Blackwood, *Expository Preaching for Today: Case Studies of Bible Passages*, p. 95; James W. Cox, *A Guide to Biblical Preaching*, p. 61; Faris D. Whitesell and Lloyd M. Perry, *Variety in Your Preaching*, p. 75; John Wood, *The Preacher's Workshop: Preparation for Expository Preaching*, p. 32.

the sermons of the prophets possessed both form and purpose. Each embodied a single theme directed toward a particular audience in order to elicit a specific response.

In the New Testament, the historian Luke presents samples of the preaching that enabled the church to penetrate the ancient world. The sermons of the apostles were without exception the proclamation of a single idea directed toward a particular audience. Donald R. Sunukjian concluded that:

> Each of Paul's messages is centered around one simple idea or thought. Each address crystallizes into a single sentence which expresses the sum and substance of the whole discourse. Everything in the sermons . . . leads up to, develops, or follows from a single unifying theme.[9]

This assessment of Paul's preaching could apply to every sermon in Acts. Each idea receives different treatment by the apostolic preacher. In Acts 2, for instance, on the day of Pentecost Peter stood before an antagonistic audience and, to gain a hearing, preached an inductive sermon. His idea is not stated until the conclusion: "Let all the house of Israel know for certain that God has made Him both Lord and Christ—this Jesus whom you crucified" (Acts 2:36 NASB). In Acts 13, on the other hand, Paul used a deductive arrangement. His major idea stands at the beginning of the sermon, and the points that follow amplify and support it. The statement found in verse 23 declares, "God, according to the promise, has brought to Israel a Savior, Jesus."

In Acts 20, when the apostle addressed the Ephesian elders, his structure was both inductive and deductive. First Paul drew from his own life an example of care for the church, then he warned in verse 28, "Be on guard for yourselves and for all the flock" (NASB). Having stated that central thought, Paul went on to explain it and apply it to the leaders seated before him. Not all the sermons in Acts develop in the same way, but each develops a central unifying concept.

9. Donald R. Sunukjian, "Patterns for Preaching: A Rhetorical Analysis of the Sermons of Paul in Acts 13, 17, and 20," p. 176.

If we preach effectively, we must know what we are about. Effective sermons major in biblical ideas brought together into an overarching unity. Having thought God's thoughts after Him, the expositor communicates and applies those thoughts to the hearers. In dependence upon the Holy Spirit, the preacher aims to confront, convict, convert, and comfort men and women through the proclamation of biblical concepts. People shape their lives and settle their eternal destinies in response to ideas.

THE DEFINITION OF AN IDEA

What do we mean by an idea? A glance at the dictionary demonstrates that defining an idea resembles trying to package fog. A complete definition could send us into the fields of philosophy, linguistics, and grammar. Webster ranges all the way from "a transcendent entity that is a real pattern of which existing things are imperfect representations" to "an entity (as a thought, concept, sensation, or image) actually or potentially present to consciousness."

The word *idea* itself moved into English from the Greek word *eido*, which means "to see" and therefore "to know." An idea sometimes enables us to see what was previously unclear. In common life when an explanation provides new insight, we exclaim, "Oh, I see what you mean!" Still another synonym for *idea* is *concept*, which comes from the verb *to conceive*. Just as a sperm and egg join to produce new life in the womb, an idea begins in the mind when things ordinarily separated come together to form a unity that either did not exist before or was not recognized previously.

The ability to abstract and synthesize, that is, to think in ideas, develops with maturity. Small children think in particulars. A child praying at breakfast thanks God for the milk, cereal, orange juice, eggs, bread, butter, and jelly, but an adult combines all these separate items into the single word *food*. An idea, therefore, may be considered a distillation of life. It abstracts out of the particulars of life what they have in common and relates them to each other. Through ideas we make sense out of the parts of our experience.

All ideas, of course, are not equally valid; we have good ideas and bad ideas. Bad ideas offer explanations of experience that do not reflect reality. They read into life what is not there. Often we embrace invalid ideas because they have not been clearly stated and therefore cannot be evaluated. In our culture, influenced as it is by mass media, we are bombarded by ridiculous concepts that are deliberately left vague so we will act without thinking.

Years ago, Marlboro cigarettes were marketed as cigarettes for sophisticated women, but Marlboro captured less than one percent of the market. Consumer research revealed, however, that men smoke because they believe it makes them more masculine; on the other hand, women smoke because they think it makes them attractive to men. As a result of these findings, the advertisers switched their campaign away from women to men and gave Marlboros a masculine image. Rugged, weather-beaten cowpunchers were portrayed smoking cigarettes as they rounded up cattle, and the theme line invited the consumer to "come to Marlboro country."

Because the association of cigarettes with cowboys conveyed the idea that smoking Marlboros makes men masculine, sales jumped four hundred percent. The idea, of course, is nonsense. Medical evidence tells us that Marlboro country is a cemetery and the Marlboro man probably suffers from cancer or lung disease. (The model for the Marlboro man did in fact die of a smoking-related disease.) Yet because the idea that "smoking makes you masculine" slipped into the mind without being clearly stated, it gained wide acceptance and boosted sales dramatically.

This is not an isolated incident. William Bryan Key, speaking about advertising, makes this unsettling statement of a Madison Avenue doctrine: "No significant belief or attitude held by any individual is apparently made on the basis of consciously perceived data." If that stands as a fundamental affirmation behind the "word from the sponsor," we should not be surprised that truth in advertising is hard to come by.

Ideas sometimes lurk in the attic of our minds like ghosts. At times we struggle to give these wispy ideas a body. "I know what I mean," we say, "but I just can't put it into words." Despite the difficulty of clothing thought with words, we have to do it. Unless ideas are expressed in words, we cannot understand, evaluate, or communicate them. If we will not—or cannot—think ourselves clear so that we say what we mean, we have no business in the pulpit. We are like a singer who can't sing, an actor who can't act, or an accountant who can't add.

THE FORMATION OF AN IDEA

To define an idea with "scrupulous exactness," we must know how ideas are formed. When reduced to its basic structure, an idea consists of only two essential elements: a *subject* and a *complement*. Both are necessary. When we talk about the subject of an idea, we mean the complete, definite answer to the question, "What am I talking about?" The subject as it is used in homiletics is not the same thing as a subject in grammar. A grammatical subject is often a single word. The subject of a sermon idea can never be only one word. It calls for the full, precise answer to the question, "What am I talking about?" Single words such as *discipleship, witnessing, worship, grief,* or *love* may masquerade as subjects, but they are too vague to be viable.

A subject cannot stand alone. By itself it is incomplete, and therefore it needs a complement. The complement "completes" the subject by answering the question, "What am I saying about what I am talking about?" A subject without a complement dangles as an open-ended question. Complements without subjects resemble automobile parts not attached to a car. An idea emerges only when the complement is joined to a definite subject.

Moreover, behind every subject there is a question either stated or implied. If I say that my subject is "the importance of faith," the implied question is, "What is the importance of faith?" "The people that God justifies . . ." forms a subject because it answers the question, "What am I talking about?" But the unstated question is, "Who are the people God justifies?" If the words *subject* and *complement* confuse you, then try thinking of the subject as a question and your complement as the answer to that question. The two together make up the idea.

An example of a subject is *the test of a person's character*. (To be precise the subject is, *What is the test of a person's character?*) That question must be completed to have meaning. We do not know what the test of character is. A variety of complements could be added to this subject to form an idea. Here are a few:

> The test of a person's character is what it takes to stop him.
>
> The test of a person's character is what he would do if he were certain no one would ever find out.
>
> The test of a person's character is like the test of an oak—how strong is he at the roots?

Each new complement tells us what is being said about the subject, and each new complement forms a different idea.

Students of preaching must search for ideas when they read sermons or prepare sermons of their own. Davis stresses that a beginner especially must give attention to the way ideas are formed:

> He must stop getting lost in the details and study the essential structure of sermons. For the time being he has to forget about the sentences, the arguments used, the quotations, the human interest stories. He has to stand off from the sermon far enough to see its shape as a whole. Stubbornly he has to ask, "What is the man really talking about, and what are the basic things he is saying about it?" This means that he must learn to distinguish between the organic structure of the idea, on the one hand, and its development on the other. It is like beginning with the skeleton in the study of anatomy.[10]

Finding the subject and complement does not start when we begin construction of our sermons. We pursue the subject and complement when we study the biblical text. Because each paragraph, section, or subsection of Scripture contains an idea, we do not understand a passage until we can state its subject and complement exactly. While other questions emerge in the struggle to

10. H. Grady Davis, *Design for Preaching*, p. 27.

understand the meaning of a biblical writer, these two ("What precisely is the author talking about?" and "What is the author saying about what he is talking about?") are fundamental.

EXAMPLES OF FORMING AN IDEA

In some biblical passages the subject and complement may be discovered with relative ease, but in others determining the idea stands as a major challenge. Psalm 117 is an example of an uncomplicated thought. The psalmist urges:

> Praise the Lord, all nations!
> Extol him, all you people!
> For his love is strong,
> His faithfulness eternal.

We do not understand the psalm until we can state its subject. What is the psalmist talking about? We might be tempted to say that the subject is praise, but praise is broad and imprecise. The psalmist isn't telling us everything about praise. Nor is the subject praise of God, which is still too broad. The subject needs more limits. The precise subject is why everyone should praise the Lord. What, then, is the psalmist saying about that? He has two complements to his subject. The Lord should be praised, first, because His love is strong and second, because His faithfulness is eternal. In this short psalm the psalmist states his naked idea, stripped of any development, but in its bare bones it has a definite subject and two complements.

Longer passages in which the idea receives extensive development can be harder to analyze for subject and complement, but the work must be done. In Hebrews 10:19–25 the author applies a previous discussion of the high-priestly work of Jesus:

> Having therefore, brethren, boldness to enter into the holy place by the blood of Jesus, by the way which he dedicated for us, a new and living way, through the veil, that is to say, his flesh; and having a great [high] priest over the house of God; let us draw near with a true heart in fullness of faith, having our hearts sprinkled

from an evil conscience: and having our body washed with pure
water, let us hold fast the confession of our hope that it waver not;
for he is faithful that promised: and let us consider one another to
provoke unto love and good works; not forsaking our own assem-
bling together, as the custom of some is, but exhorting one another; and so much the more, as ye see the day drawing nigh.
(ASV)

While many details in this passage demand explanation, a
careful student will distinguish the trunk from the branches.
Until a subject emerges, it is not possible to determine the value
or significance of anything else that is said. A casual reader might
be tempted to state the subject as the high priesthood of Jesus,
but that subject covers too much. The author of Hebrews does
not tell his readers everything about Christ's high-priestly work
in this single paragraph. Nor is the text talking about boldness to
enter the holy place, which is actually a sub-idea in the passage.

The subject can always be stated as a question. Therefore, the
subject can be narrowed to, "What should happen because believers can enter into God's presence with confidence and have
a great high priest?" The complements of this subject will be a series of results, and there are three. First, they should draw near
to God with the assurance that comes from a cleansed heart and
life; second, they should hold unswervingly to the hope they
profess; and third, they should spur on one another to love and
good works. Everything else in this paragraph enlarges on this
subject with its complements.

Look at how the process works with the poetry in an Old Testament book. The small diary of Habakkuk consists of a series of
conversations that the prophet had with God. In the opening
chapter, Habakkuk is upset with God for not punishing evil in
the nation of Judah and in the broader world. We must first state
the ideas that make up the argument the prophet had with God.

Habakkuk opens with a complaint in 1:2–4. Stated as a subject
and complement, this is the idea:

- *Subject*: What is Habakkuk's lament about the injustice he
  sees in Judah?

- *Complement*: He wonders why God, who is righteous, doesn't judge the nation for its sin.
- *Idea*: Habakkuk laments that his righteous God does not punish sin in Judah.

God replies to the prophet in 1:5–7. God's answer can also be stated as a subject and complement:
- *Subject*: How will God bring judgment on Judah?
- *Complement*: God will use the wicked Babylonians to punish His people.
- *Idea*: God will use the wicked Babylonians to punish His people.

Note that both of these paragraphs (1:2–11) can now be joined in a larger subject and complement:
- *Subject*: How will God punish the evil and injustice rampant in His people, Judah?
- *Complement*: God will use the wicked Babylonians as His whipping stick.
- *Idea*: God will judge the evil in His own people, Judah, through an invasion by the wicked Babylonians.

That leads us, then, to the third paragraph in the passage found in 1:12–2:1:
- *Subject*: How could a righteous God use the evil and godless Babylon to punish a more righteous nation like Judah?
- *Complement*: God will also punish the Babylonians at an appointed time.
- *Idea*: Even though God will use the wicked Babylonians to punish Judah, He will also judge the Babylonians for their sin.

There are many images used in the poetry of this chapter, but they must be separated from the ideas they support. It is important to go through the process of stating the subject and complement to get at the ideas. Ideas are slippery creatures that can easily escape your grasp.

In each of these passages, we determined the subject and its complement(s) to discover the *structure* of the idea. In order to think clearly, we must constantly distinguish the idea from the way the idea develops. The effort to state the idea of a passage and then to state the idea of our sermon in exact words can be frustrating and irritating, but in the long run it is the most economical use of our time. What is more important, we cannot get anywhere without doing it. We do not understand what we are reading unless we can clearly express the subject and complement of the section we are studying. And those who hear us preach do not understand what we are saying unless they can answer the basic questions: What were we talking about today? What were we saying about what we were talking about? Yet Sunday after Sunday men and women leave church unable to state the preacher's basic idea because the preacher has not bothered to state it in the sermon. When people leave church in a mental fog, they do so at their spiritual peril.

Thinking is difficult, but it stands as our essential work. Make no mistake about the difficulty of the task. It is often slow, discouraging, overwhelming. But when God calls us to preach, He calls us to love Him with our minds. God deserves that kind of love and so do the people to whom we minister.

On a cold, gloomy morning a preacher worked on his sermon from breakfast until noon with little to show for his labor. Impatiently he laid down his pen and looked disconsolately out the window, feeling sorry for himself because his sermons came so slowly. Then there flashed into his mind an insight that had profound effect on his later ministry. "Your fellow Christians," he thought, "will spend far more time on this sermon than you will. They come from a hundred homes. They travel hundreds of miles in the aggregate to be in the service. They will spend three hundred hours participating in the worship and listening to what you have to say. Don't complain about the hours you are spending in preparation and the agony you experience. The people deserve all you can give them."

New Concepts

Idea
Two essential elements in the statement of an idea:
    subject
    complement

Definitions

Idea—a distillation of life that abstracts out of the particulars of experience what they have in common and relates them to each other.

Subject—the complete, definite answer to the question, "What am I talking about?"

Complement—the answer to the question, "What exactly am I saying about what I'm talking about?"

Exercises

Determine the subject and complement in the following paragraphs:

1. A good sermon leaves you wondering how the preacher knew all about you.

   Subject: _____

   Complement: _____

   _____

2. Today's pulpit has lost its authority because it has largely ignored the Bible as the source of its message.

   Subject: _____

   Complement: _____

   _____

3. The young have lots of time and few memories while the elderly have lots of memories and little time.

Subject: _____

Complement: _____

_____

4. The popular saying has it, "Charity begins at home." It doesn't. Charity begins where love connects with need.

Subject: _____

Complement: _____

_____

5. Attention Teenagers: If you are tired of being hassled by unreasonable parents, now is the time for action. Leave home now and pay your own way while you still know everything.

Subject: _____

Complement: _____

_____

6. "Not everyone who says to me, 'Lord, Lord,' will enter the kingdom of heaven, but only he who does the will of my Father who is in heaven." (Matthew 7:21)

Subject: _____

Complement: _____

_____

7. "Remember your Creator in the days of your youth before the days of trouble come and the years approach when you say, 'I find no pleasure in them.'" (Ecclesiastes 12:1)

    Subject: _____

    Complement: _____

    _____

8. "Do not speak harshly to a man older than yourself, but advise him as you would your own father; treat the younger men as brothers and older women as you would your mother. Always treat younger women with propriety, as if they were your sisters." (1 Timothy 5: 1–3)

    Subject: _____

    Complement: _____

    _____

9. Forgiveness "cannot mean that we cover up a fault with a 'mantle of charity.' Divine things are never an illusion and deception. On the contrary, before the sin is forgiven the mantle with which it is covered must be removed. The sin must be unmercifully—yes unmercifully—exposed to the light of God's countenance (Psalm 90)." (Helmut Thielicke)

    Subject: _____

    Complement: _____

    _____

10. "Blessed is the person
    whose transgressions are forgiven,
    whose sins are covered.
    Blessed is the person
    whose sin the Lord does not count against him
    And in whose spirit is no deceit." (Psalm 32:1–2)

    Subject: _____

    Complement: _____

    _____

(Answers are in appendix 1.)

three

TOOLS
of the Trade

It is difficult to think. It is more difficult to think about thinking. It is most difficult to talk about thinking about thinking. Yet that stands as the basic task of homiletics. Homileticians observe how preachers work and attempt to get inside their heads to discover what goes on there as they prepare to preach. Then they must describe the process clearly enough to make sense to a student. The assignment borders on the impossible.

51

Whom should homileticians study? Certainly not every preacher. There are duffers in the pulpit as well as on the golf course. To discover how to do something well, we usually study those who are effective in what they do. Yet well-known pulpiteers who write "how I do it" books reveal as many variations in procedure as there are authors. More baffling perhaps are the non-methods supposedly used by some effective preachers. These ministers who "speak from a full heart" or "share" sometimes insist that while they have abandoned the rules, their sermons still hit the target. Such preaching has to be reckoned with. As professional skills go, sermon construction ranks among the most inexact when compared, say, with cooking spaghetti, removing an appendix, or flying an airplane.

How do we evaluate the assortment of approaches or explain the apparent effectiveness of sermons that appear to have behind them no method at all? More to the point, how do we derive procedures from all of this that others may follow?

For one thing, we are concerned with expository preaching, and ministers whose preaching is shaped by the Bible possess more in common than preachers in general. In addition, expositors who claim they follow no rules usually have not analyzed how they study. Whatever we do regularly becomes our method even if we have come to it intuitively, and few effective expositors are as devoid of method as they sometimes claim. Furthermore, to analyze how to do something well, we are drawn to those who do it well consistently, not those who do it well by chance now and then. Clear, relevant biblical exposition does not take place Sunday after Sunday by either intuition or accident. Good expositors have methods for their study.

Two conclusions emerge from the fact that expositors go about their work in different ways. First, detailed instruction about how to think may sometimes get in the way of the process. The damage instruction can do is reflected in the story of a lawyer and physician who regularly played golf together. They were evenly matched and enjoyed a keen sense of rivalry. Then one spring the lawyer's game improved so much that the doctor was losing regularly. The doctor's attempts to better his own game were unsuccessful, but then he came up with an idea. At a bookstore he bought three how-to-play-golf manuals and sent them to the lawyer for a birthday present. It wasn't long before they were evenly matched again.

Second, thinking is a dynamic process. Effective biblical preaching requires insight, imagination, and spiritual sensitivity—none of which comes from merely following directions. When a discussion on how to prepare an expository sermon resembles instructions on how to build a doghouse, something has gone wrong. Building the expository sermon comes nearer to erecting cathedrals than hammering together animal shelters. But even cathedral builders have their way of doing things. While it requires a lifetime with the Scriptures and with people to do mature exposition, the apprentice needs specific help on how to begin. Knowing how others work in the Bible can be welcome assistance. To this counsel we must each bring our own mind, spirit, and experience, and out of repeated practice in the strenuous work of thinking, we must develop our own way of working. But an awareness of how others approach the task produces confidence and contributes to a more efficient use of time and energy.

Throughout the discussion on how to develop an expository sermon, therefore, it should be kept in mind that while the stages for preparation are treated in sequence, they sometimes mix. For example, the logical time to prepare an introduction comes when the development of the entire sermon has become clear. Experienced preachers, though, sometimes stumble across a workable lead for an introduction early in their preparation. They take it whenever they can get it, though they may wait until near the end of their work to fit it to the sermon.

What, then, are the stages in the preparation of the expository sermon?

Stage 1 Choose the passage to be preached.

An old recipe for a rabbit stew starts out, "First catch the rabbit." That puts first things first. Without the rabbit there is no dish. The obvious first questions confronting us are: What shall I talk about? From what passage of Scripture should I draw my sermon?

These questions need not be faced on a Monday morning six days before the sermon delivery. A conscientious ministry in the Scriptures depends on thoughtful planning for the entire year. Those who use the lectionary have passages chosen for them. The decision they must make is which particular passage from the Old or New Testament they will focus on. Those who are not in the traditions that use a lectionary can save time by investing time in a preaching calendar. Sometime before their year begins, they force themselves to decide Sunday by Sunday, service by service, what passage they will preach.

While all Scripture is profitable, not every Scripture possesses equal profit for a congregation at a particular time. Preachers' insight and concern will be reflected in what biblical truths they offer to their people. In their ministry, expositors serve as builders of bridges as they endeavor to span the gulf between the Word of God and the concerns of men and women. To do this they must be as familiar with the needs of their churches as they are with the content of their Bibles. While they relate the Scriptures to their people's lives in individual sermons, they know the importance of a preaching calendar that chooses broad topics or passages of Scripture that speak to the needs of their particular congregation.

THOUGHT UNITS

Often we will work our way chapter by chapter, verse by verse, through different books of the Bible. In making our calendar, therefore, we will read through the books several times and then divide them into portions that we will expound in particular sermons. In doing this, we should select the passages based on the natural literary divisions of the material. We will not count out ten or twelve verses to a sermon as though each verse could be handled as a separate thought. Instead, we will search for the biblical writer's ideas. For example, in the New Testament letters, the texts will usually be selected by paragraph divisions, because paragraphs delineate the building blocks of thought. As expositors, we will usually choose one or more of these paragraphs to expound, depending on how they relate to one another and thus to one of the author's major ideas.

Of course, no divine hand fashioned those paragraph divisions. The indentations in our translations reflect the decisions of editors who have attempted to mark out shifts of thought in the original. Consequently, paragraph divisions in one translation may differ from those in another. As a general rule, older translations tend toward longer, heavier paragraphs than do our more modern translations, which emphasize readability and eye appeal. Even the Hebrew and Greek texts reflect editorial variations in the paragraph divisions. Yet all efforts at paragraphing are based on the development and transition of thought. Diligent expositors will examine the paragraph breakdowns in both the original texts and the English translations, select the divisions of the material that seem to be the most logical, and use them as the basis of their expositions.

If we are working within narrative sections, however, we will more likely deal with a literary unit larger than a paragraph or two. For example, when exploring an episode such as David's adultery with Bathsheba, we would violate the story were we to preach it a paragraph at a time. Instead, we would probably base the sermon on the entire eleventh chapter of 2 Samuel and at least part of the twelfth, because this entire section of 2 Samuel records David's sin and its devastating consequences.

In poetic literature such as the Psalms, a paragraph roughly equals the stanza or strophe of a poem. While at times we may choose to expound only a single stanza, normally we will treat the entire psalm. In selecting passages for the expository sermon, therefore, a general principle to follow is this: *Base the sermon on a literary unit of biblical thought.*

Working in the book of Proverbs, however, presents a special challenge to this rule. While the opening nine chapters can be divided into units of thought that are relatively easy to identify, the sayings found in chapters 10 through 31 seem to be a collection of pithy, seemingly unconnected sentences. Preaching on the proverbs one after the other, however, will turn the sermon into buckshot. Because of this, messages preached from Proverbs usually handle the sayings by topics. Several are taken from different chapters and are put together in a logical or psychological sequence that forms the units of thought for the sermon. Derek Kidner suggests eight of these subject studies in his brief commentary on the book.[1]

We should note, however, that recent commentators on Proverbs point up linguistic connections between the proverbs in the Hebrew text that suggest the proverbs may not be as random as they might first appear.[2]

TOPICAL EXPOSITION

As expositors, we may normally work our way through entire biblical books or extended passages in Scripture. Yet at some time or another during the year, we will preach on topics. Sermons preached at Easter and at Christmas require special topical treatment. In addition we may preach on theological topics such as the Trinity, reconciliation, worship, God's concern for the poor, or the authority of the Scriptures. In dealing with a Christian doctrine, we may begin our study of the Scriptures with the help of an analytical concordance or a topical Bible. The index in books on theology can direct us to discussions of the subject and passages of Scripture on which the doctrine is based.

At times, we may also want to speak to personal concerns, such as guilt, grief, forgiveness, loneliness, jealousy, marriage, and divorce. Preaching on personal problems, sometimes called life-situation preaching, poses a particular difficulty. How do we find the passage or passages to preach? If we have a broad knowledge of the Scriptures, we will be aware of passages that deal with people with those problems. We will know the temptation

1. Derek Kidner, *The Proverbs: An Introduction and Commentary* (Downers Grove, Ill.: InterVarsity, 1969).

2. See, for example, Bruce Waltke's exposition of Proverbs 26:1–12 in *The Big Idea of Biblical Preaching*, eds. Keith Willhite and Scott Gibson; or idem., "Proverbs 10:1–16: A Coherent Collection?" in *Reading and Hearing the Word from Text to Sermon: Essays in Honor of John H. Stek*, ed. Arie C. Leder (Grand Rapids: Calvin Theological Seminary and CRC Publications, 1998).

of Adam, the jealousy of Cain, the guilty conscience of Jacob, the depression of Elijah, or the teaching of Jesus about the need to confront and to forgive someone who has offended us. If we do not have that broad grasp of Scripture, a concordance may supply workable leads. In addition, books wrestling with moral and ethical issues from a Christian perspective may not only analyze the problem but also suggest biblical material to be considered. In topical exposition, therefore, we begin with a subject or a problem and then look for a passage or passages that relate to it.

Topical exposition faces two problems. First, the topic we are considering may be dealt with in several passages of the Scripture. Each of the individual passages, therefore, must be examined in its context. Isolating a single passage on which to base a teaching may ignore tensions built into the biblical record. Usually, topical exposition takes more study than exposition based on a single passage.

An additional problem in topical exposition is that we may read something into the scriptural account in order to read something significant out of it. Starting with personal problems poses the particular danger of misusing the Scriptures. If the difficulty of starting with the Bible is that we may never get to the twenty-first century, then the trap of starting with the twenty-first century is that we may deal dishonestly with the Bible. In our eagerness to say something helpful to hurting people, we may end up saying what the Bible is not saying at all. We can use texts of Scripture that we feel support what we want to say without considering the intent of the biblical author or the context of the verses. Those who want to address the felt needs of their people are to be commended for their desire to be relevant. At the same time, there is no greater betrayal of our calling than putting words in God's mouth.

However we select the passage, we must allow it to speak for itself. Often a passage will not say what we expected it to say. We may resort to "proof texts" for favorite doctrines by completely ignoring the context in which these texts lie. We may be tempted to transform biblical authors into modern psychologists by saying in a sermon what they never intended. Topical exposition differs from the so-called topical sermon, therefore, in that the thought of the Scripture shapes all that is said in defining and developing the topic.

SERMON LENGTH

Another factor we must consider in choosing what to preach is time. We must preach our sermons in a limited number of minutes. Few congregations being offered well-prepared and attractively presented biblical truth will sit before their pastor with stopwatches in their hands. Yet, if we're honest, we will not take time not granted to us. We must tailor our sermons to our time, and the cutting should be done in the study rather than in the pulpit.

If you are in a congregation that allows only twelve to fifteen minutes for the sermon, you may still do exposition. You are limited, of course, in the length of the passage you can present and the detail with which you develop it. You will be limited, perhaps, to the major idea of the section, and in a few strokes, show the congregation how that idea comes from the passage and applies to life.

Even if you are allowed forty-five minutes for your sermons, you must still make choices. You can seldom tell your people all you have discovered about a passage, nor should you try. Whether you have fifteen minutes or an hour, therefore, you must choose what to include or exclude in a particular sermon. Through experience you can discover the length of a passage you may treat in detail. You also sense when you must settle for a bird's-eye view of a passage rather than a worm's-eye analysis. Both the units of thought and the time allowed to cover them, therefore, must be considered when you select a passage to be preached.

Stage 2   Study your passage and gather your notes.

Our task begins with studying the passage and recording our findings. There are several things we should consider.

THE CONTEXT

Having selected the passage, we must first examine it in its context. The passage does not exist in isolation. As individual verses rest within a paragraph, the paragraphs are part of a chapter, and the chapters are part of the book. If you were reading any other book, you would not open it to page 50, read a paragraph, and from that, assume that you could speak with some authority about the author's meaning. The author may be giving you the argument of an opponent, not his own. At the very least, you would want to read the whole chapter to discover how this one paragraph fits within the larger section. If you really want to understand your paragraph, you would also ask questions about how the chapter that contains your paragraph fits within the entire book. The old saw still has a sharp edge: "The text without the context is a pretext."

For this reason, we begin our study of a biblical passage by relating it to the broader literary unit of which it is a part. Usually this demands that we read the book several times and in different translations. Even if we have skills in reading Hebrew or Greek, we usually find it easier to map out the broad developments of an author's thought by reading it in English. Scores of different versions are available, ranging from literal, word-for-word translations like those in interlinears (where English words are placed under the Hebrew or Greek text) to versions that present the Scriptures in contemporary language.

Different translations serve us in different ways. We can gain an impression of the sharpness and vitality of the original Hebrew or Greek by reading different kinds of translations. For example, as a study Bible we may use the New American Standard Bible, which stays close to the original but may sound stiff and wooden when read in public. The New King James Version is also closer to the original texts. Others who like to be faithful to the past prefer the King James Version. Other translations and paraphrases catch the dynamic equivalent of the original text and reflect the ideas of the biblical author, for example, Eugene Peterson's *The Message*, J. B. Phillips's paraphrase of the New Testament, or the New Living Translation. A translation that searches for the middle ground between allegiance to the Hebrew or Greek and a sensitive feeling for style is the New International Version. By using these translations and others, we can understand the broad context of the passage.

Setting our passage within its wider framework, therefore, simply gives the Bible the same chance we give the author of a novel. We want to fit our paragraph into its wider unit of thought. We do not have to find this framework by ourselves. Introductions to the Old or New Testament and introductory sections of commentaries usually discuss why a book was written and outline its contents. While commentators sometimes disagree on these matters, we can consider their frameworks as we read through the Scripture for ourselves.

Not only should our passage be placed within the broader unity of the book, but it must also be related to its immediate context. More clues to meaning come from a study of the surrounding context than from an examination of details within a passage. To understand a paragraph or subsection, we must explain how it develops out of what precedes it and relates to what follows it. Would it make any difference if this particular passage were not there? What purpose does this passage serve in the book? To understand 1 Corinthians 13, for instance, we must understand that it is part of a larger unit dealing with spiritual gifts in chapters 12–14. These chapters must be considered together to interpret the contrast of love with spiritual gifts in chapter 13. In addition, earlier chapters of the Corinthian letter reveal the spiritual condition of the readers and make us reflect on how love would apply in their situation.

As you read the passage in different translations, do so with a pen in hand. Write out as precisely as possible the problems you have in understanding the passage. Write them all down—make yourself state them. If different translations disagree significantly, note that. It usually means that the translators look at the passage from different points of view. Try to state the differences. It's possible that what confuses you is unfamiliar background or unknown figures of speech. You may not follow the author's thought because it is tightly reasoned. Asking the right questions becomes an essential step in finding the right answers.

Remember that you're looking for the author's ideas. Begin by stating in rough fashion what you think the writer is talking about—that is, his *subject*. Then try to determine what major assertion(s) the biblical writer is making *about* the subject, that is, the *complement(s)*.

If you cannot state a subject at this point, what is hindering you from doing so?

- Is there a verse that doesn't seem to fit?
- Is the writer assuming a connection between his assertions that you need to state?
- Is it that you can't figure out how this paragraph relates to what precedes or follows it?
- Is there an image the author uses that you don't understand?

It's one thing not to know, but another thing not to know what you don't know. Uncovering the questions you have and writing them down can help you get at the author's subject.

Having placed the passage within its context, you must now examine its details. In the Epistles and in parts of the Gospels, this means examining the vocabulary and the grammatical structure of the passage. In narrative passages you will look for statements by the author that explain what is taking place. For example, in 2 Samuel 11, the historian reports on the sin of David without judgment. Only at the end of the chapter does he comment that "what David did displeased the Lord." Where there are no editorial comments, you must ask questions like, "Why did the biblical author include this episode?" or "Are there details in the passage that, at first, seem extraneous?" The authors of the Old Testament are superb storytellers, but they are also theologians. They are not simply giving us stories to tell our children at bedtime; they are telling us their stories to give us truth about God.

It's amazing how much of the Bible you can learn by simply reading it in English, but some knowledge of the original languages does give you an advantage. Reading a passage in Hebrew or Greek resembles watching a film on DVD compared to ordi-

Stage Two

nary television. Both give you the same picture, but DVD adds vividness and precision. You need not be an expert in the Hebrew or Greek languages to use them with benefit, and almost anyone can use some of the available linguistic tools. Accuracy, as well as integrity, demands that we develop every possible skill to keep us from declaring in the name of God what the Holy Spirit never intended to convey.

Up to this point, we have been looking at the biblical text itself, both in English and possibly in the original languages, to try to determine the overall idea of the passage by asking questions to clarify what we do not understand. Now we can use tools to help us dig into the passage. At least six different aids are available to help us as we examine our text.

LEXICONS

A lexicon serves as a kind of dictionary for the original languages. Through using a lexicon we can find definitions of a word as it is used in Hebrew or Greek. But it is more than a dictionary: along with the definition of a word, it gives us root meanings, identification of some grammatical forms, a list of passages where the word occurs, classification of its uses in its various contexts, and some illustrations that help give color to the word.

CONCORDANCES

While lexicons, like dictionaries, define words, sometimes it is essential to study a word in the passages where it occurs. To determine the meaning of words through usage, we use a concordance.

GRAMMARS

But meaning does not come from words alone. Words must be understood as they are used in phrases, clauses, sentences, and paragraphs. A study of syntax examines how words com-

Stage Two

bine to render meaning, and grammars assist us in that study. Not only does a grammar offer general help in describing how words are formed and put together in sentences, but those with an index to Scripture often give insight into particular passages being studied.

WORD-STUDY BOOKS

Much of the work of evaluating how biblical writers use words has been done for us by scholars. Word-study books provide us with insights into words used throughout the Old and New Testaments, and because words are stupid things until placed in a context, these books deal with their grammatical use when appropriate.

BIBLE DICTIONARIES AND ENCYCLOPEDIAS

Unlike most of our English dictionaries, Bible dictionaries offer more than a definition of a word. They give us brief discussions of people, events, and backgrounds of the biblical material. Many of your questions about when or where a book was written, its readers, and its author will be answered by a good Bible dictionary or encyclopedia. Because different reference works display different strengths, an examination of the same subject in several different encyclopedias and dictionaries enables you to achieve both balance and completeness. In addition, through the use of bibliographies found at the end of each article, you can pursue a topic to even greater depth.

COMMENTARIES

As you teach the Scriptures, you need teachers to teach you. Through commentaries, scholars serve the church. They offer a wealth of information about the meaning of words, backgrounds of passages, and the argument of a writer. As a general rule, it is wiser (and cheaper!) to select the best volumes on individual Bible books from several different series. It is also helpful to consult an

Stage Two

assortment of commentaries on a passage and weigh what they say against each other in determining the meaning of the biblical author. For your basic study, you will want to consult commentaries based on the original languages and not only on the English text. Several bibliographies exist to guide you in your selection of a library.

For your initial study you will be helped by consulting commentaries based on the original languages. Volumes in the International Critical Commentary series or the Word Biblical Commentary series are examples of this category. These are often quite technical and require some knowledge of the original languages, but they wrestle with the meaning of the text.

You will also want to consult expositional commentaries. They are much more English-friendly, but be sure to select those written by authors who work from the original languages. InterVarsity's Tyndale Old Testament Commentary series or Zondervan's Expositor's Bible Commentary series would be typical of this group.

You will find additional help in commentaries that focus on application, such as the NIV Application Commentaries in both the Old and New Testaments or the IVP New Testament Commentaries. These volumes also deal with exegesis and exposition, but sometimes not at the same depth as the critical or expositional commentaries.

There are many books and tapes of sermons preached by well-known preachers. Although these may give you some ideas of how to approach or apply your sermon, they should not be used early in your preparation. You will be tempted to rely too heavily on them and therefore short-circuit your own study of the text.

BIBLIOGRAPHIES

An excellent resource for building your library is the *Commentary and Reference Survey* compiled by John Glynn (Dallas: s.n., 1995). Glynn offers helpful advice for building a "bare-bones" personal reference library. He suggests books and computer programs for three different groups: informed laypeople, Bible col-

Stage Two

lege and seminary students, and pastors. In addition to recommending reference books for your personal library, Glynn evaluates 750 commentary series and individual commentaries for single books of the Bible. He bases his judgments on published bibliographies and surveys, reviews in theological journals, and recommendations from recognized scholars. Glynn's survey answers the question, "What volumes should I purchase to get the best books for my bucks?"

Seminary bookstores can also help you to build a basic library or suggest the best commentaries on individual books of the Bible. Some seminaries have bibliographies compiled by their faculty of the best volumes to purchase. A library is indispensable for anyone doing serious Bible study. A collection of basic study books and some good commentaries will cost about as much as a year's tuition at many colleges or seminaries, but if selected with care, their value will last a lifetime.

OTHER TOOLS

Today we are benefited by having computers and study aids on CD-ROM. They put at our fingertips a library including the Greek and Hebrew text, English translations of the Bible, concordances, commentaries (both ancient and modern), and word study aids, all keyed to particular passages. Even more impressive, these programs are highly interactive and allow us to move back and forth between the biblical text and the tools of scholarship.

In my own study, I use a legal-size pad to record the results of my study. For passages covering only a few verses, I devote a separate page to each verse. For larger sections of text, for example, in the stories of the Old Testament, I may devote a page to an entire paragraph. I will have separate sheets for notes about the idea and its development, possible illustrations, and possible leads on introductions and applications. Admittedly, this is the confession of a dinosaur. Many ministers use a computer to keep track of all this information. However you do it, you need a place to record your findings.

Stage Two

In studying the details of the passage and placing it in its context, we are already moving into the next stage.

Stage 3   As you study the passage, relate the parts to each other to determine the exegetical idea and its development.

Our linguistic and grammatical analyses must never become an end in themselves, but rather should lead to a clearer understanding of the passage as a whole. The process resembles an hourglass that moves from synthesis to analysis and back to synthesis. Initially we read the passage and its context in English to understand the author's meaning. Then through analysis we test our initial impressions through an examination of the details. After that we come to a final statement of the subject and complement in the light of that study.

Throughout the process you will ask, "Exactly what is the biblical writer talking about?" When you have a possible subject, go back through the passage and relate the subject to the details.

- Does the subject fit all the parts?
- Is it too broad? How would you narrow it?
- Is it too narrow? Is there a larger subject that accounts for all the parts?
- Is your subject an exact description of what the passage is talking about?

THE SUBJECT

The initial statement of a subject will often be too broad. To narrow it, try testing your subject with a series of definitive questions. A bit of verse tells us what those questions are:

> I had six faithful friends,
> They taught me all I knew,
> Their names are How and What and Why,
> When and Where and Who.

Remember, your subject can always be stated in the form of a question. Applying these six questions to your proposed subject, therefore, will help you be more exact. Take as a case in point James 1:5–8:

> If any of you lacks wisdom, let him ask of God, who gives to all men generously and without reproach, and it will be given to him. But he must ask in faith without any doubting, for the one who doubts is like the surf of the sea, driven and tossed by the wind. For that man ought not to expect that he will receive anything from the Lord, being a double-minded man, unstable in all his ways. (NASB)

Our initial response to this paragraph might be that James is talking about wisdom. While wisdom emerges as a major element in the passage, it is much too broad a subject because James does not discuss what wisdom is, why we need it, or when we need it. Looking at the passage more closely, we find he is talking about "how to obtain wisdom," a more precise statement of the subject. An awareness of the immediate context, however, enables us to limit the subject even further. The preceding paragraph, verses 2–4, demonstrates that joy is the proper response to trials, and our paragraph extends that discussion. Therefore, a more complete subject for James 1:5–8 would be "how to obtain wisdom in the midst of trials." All the details in the paragraph, directly or indirectly, relate to that subject. When a proposed subject accurately describes what the author is talking about, it illuminates the details of the passage; and the subject, in turn, will be illuminated by the details.

THE COMPLEMENT

Having isolated the subject, you must now determine the complement, or complements, that *complete* the subject and make it into an idea. In doing this you must become aware of the structure of the passage and distinguish between its major and supporting assertions. Often the complement becomes immediately obvious once you have stated the subject. In James 1:5–8 the complement to the subject "how to obtain wisdom in the midst of trials," is "ask God for it in faith." The complete statement of the idea, then, merely joins the subject with the complement: "Wisdom in trials is obtained by asking God for it in faith." Everything else in the paragraph supports or elaborates that idea.

Particularly in passages found in the letters of the New Testament, the biblical writers often weave tightly reasoned arguments. The ideas may be uncovered through the use of a mechanical layout. Such a layout points up the relationship of the dependent clauses to the independent clauses. Diagramming, a more demanding method for unraveling structure, determines the relationship of individual words within sentences. A mechanical layout or diagram may be based on either the original text or an English translation. Either a diagram or a mechanical layout brings analysis and synthesis together so that the major idea of a passage is separated from its supporting material.

While the letters in the New Testament make a fundamental contribution to Christian theology, they constitute only one of many literary forms found in the Bible. The Scriptures contain many types of literature such as parables, poetry, proverbs, prayers, speeches, allegories, history, laws, contracts, biography, drama, apocalypse, and stories. To find the idea in any of them, we must be aware of the kind of literature we are reading and the conventions that are unique to it. We do not interpret poems as we do legal contracts. A parable differs significantly from a historical narrative or a love song. When working in narrative literature, we seldom have to work through a maze of complex grammatical relationships, but instead we derive the author's meaning from a broad study of several paragraphs.

A series of different questions must be raised when trying to understand a story. A sampling of those questions might be:

- Who are the characters in the story and why did the author include them?
- Do the characters contrast with one another?
- How do these characters develop as the story develops?
- What does the setting contribute to the story?

Stage Three

- What structure holds the story together and provides its unity?
- How do the individual episodes fit into the total framework?
- What conflicts develop and how are they resolved?
- Why did the writer bother telling the story?
- What ideas lie behind the story that may be implied but not stated?
- Can those ideas be stated through a subject and complement?

Much of the Old Testament is poetic in form. In reading translations that print poetry as poetry and not as prose, we discover that poetry is the most-used literary form in Old Testament literature. Even sections we ordinarily think of as prose (history, prophecy, wisdom literature) contain large amounts of poetry. Poets do not usually tell stories, but instead express feelings and reflections about life. In Hebrew literature poets communicate through parallelism that repeats, contrasts, or adds to the previous thoughts, and they use figurative language that may not be true to fact but is true to feelings. Images and figures of speech give more life and force to speech because they join experience to fact. When farmers observe that "the land needs rain," they are true to fact, but if they say that "the earth thirsts for rain," they are true to both fact and feeling. Poets major in structures and language to add force and depth to what they are saying. Therefore interpreting poetry raises its own set of questions:

- What meanings lie behind the images and figures of speech?
- What feelings does the poet express by the choice of language?
- What elements of form and structure does the poet use to discipline thought?
- What would be lost if the same truth were presented in prose?

Stage Three

In whatever genre of literature you study, you will not only try to determine the writer's idea, but you will also want to discern how the idea is developed in the passage. Take your statement of the idea (subject joined to complement) and run it back over the passage. Can you explain how the parts fit your idea? The author may not develop a psalm in a logical order, but there may be a psychological relationship. Have you identified that? The storyteller tells the story, but if there are details in the narrative that don't seem to contribute to the story, ask yourself why. The Bible is great literature. It speaks to our minds and to our emotions. As great literature, it does not deal in unnecessary trivia. The authors want us to get and to feel what they are writing about. When they include details, they do so for a purpose. If you have uncovered the author's idea, then the different parts of the passage should illuminate it. It is often in the parts that we don't immediately understand that some of the best insights can be found.

One device you may find helpful is to paraphrase the passage in your own words. Be exact in thought, and carefully state the relationships you see within the text whether the biblical writer explicitly states them or not. As you write, you may have to alter the statement of your exegetical idea to fit the parts of the passage. Don't bend the passage to fit your statement of the idea.

At this point, as a result of your study, you should be able to do two things: first, to state the idea of the passage in a single sentence that combines your subject and complement; and second, to state how the parts of the passage relate to the idea.

This is sweaty, difficult work, but it has to be done.

Stage Three

New Concepts

Context
Lexicon
Concordance
Bible dictionary and encyclopedia
Mechanical layout
Diagramming
Paraphrase of a passage

Definitions

Bible dictionary and encyclopedia—contain articles on a wide variety of biblical subjects, including background of Bible books and biographies of biblical characters.

Concordance—helps determine the meaning of words through usage.

Context—the wider framework in which a passage occurs. It can be as narrow as a paragraph or chapter, but it ultimately includes the larger argument of the book.

Diagramming—shows the relationship of individual words within sentences as well as the relationship of the clauses.

Lexicon—provides definitions, root meanings, identification of some grammatical forms, a list of passages in which a word occurs, classifications of the use of a word in its various contexts, and some illustrations that help give color to a word.

Mechanical layout—shows the relationship of the dependent and independent clauses in a paragraph.

Paraphrase of a passage—states the progression of ideas in a passage in contemporary language.

For Further Reading

Different types *(genres)* of literature require different mind-sets to appreciate them. You don't read a legal document in the same way you read a novel or a poem or a letter from your insurance company. Make time to read *How to Read the Bible for All It's Worth* by

Gordon Fee and Douglas Stuart (Grand Rapids: Zondervan, 1993). It is an easy-to-understand guide to help you ask the right questions in your endeavor to interpret and apply the Scriptures accurately.

There are ten helpful chapters on preaching the different sections and the different genres of the Scripture in *The Handbook of Contemporary Preaching* (Nashville: Broadman, 1992) that may also help you tackle the different types of literature in the Bible.

A major genre in the Bible is narrative. A very practical treatment of how to study Old Testament narrative is by Steve Mathewson (*The Art of Preaching Old Testament Narrative* [Grand Rapids: Baker, forthcoming]). Mathewson is sympathetic to the readers who may be trying to find their way through the biblical stories. At the same time, he gives helpful guidelines for those who know the basics already and want to learn more.

If you're willing to struggle a bit, then tackle Robert Alter's book *The Art of Biblical Narrative* (New York: Basic Books, 1981). He approaches the stories of the Old Testament from the perspective of a literary critic. His book is based on the Hebrew text; nevertheless, thoughtful readers who do not know Hebrew can still profit from reading it. Alter has also written *The Art of Biblical Poetry* (New York: Basic Books, 1987), which does for poetry what his first book did for narrative.

Another helpful book, written by friends of mine, fleshes out the principles of this chapter. It is *The Big Idea of Biblical Preaching*, edited by Keith Willhite and Scott Gibson (Grand Rapids: Baker, 1998). In one chapter, Bruce Waltke deals with how a study of poetics can unlock the central thought of broader passages in the Proverbs. He uses Proverbs 26:1–12 as a test case. In another chapter, Paul Borden spells out in detail how a preacher finds and communicates the great idea in a biblical story.

Another insightful discussion of the literary forms in the Scripture is by Leland Ryken in *A Complete Literary Guide to the Bible* (Grand Rapids: Zondervan, 1993). Ryken, who loves great literature, reminds us that while the Bible differs from other books, it must be read like other books. It should be approached not simply as a textbook on theology, but as literature.

four

THE ROAD
from Text to Sermon

Expository sermons consist of ideas drawn from the Scriptures, but the ideas of Scripture must be related to life. To preach effectively, therefore, expositors must be involved in three different worlds: the world of the Bible, the modern world, and the particular world in which we are called to preach.

Up to now, in our study we have entered the world of the Bible. God chose to reveal

Himself within history to nations that can be located on a map. These nations were enveloped in cultures as developed as our own. They used languages that can be described in grammars. We must first try to understand what the revelation of God meant for the men and women to whom it was originally given.

A second world we must consider is the modern world. We must be aware of the currents swirling across our own times. Each generation develops out of its own history and culture and speaks its own language. We may stand before a congregation and deliver exegetically accurate sermons that are scholarly and organized, but they are dead and powerless because they ignore the life-wrenching problems and questions of our hearers. Such sermons, spoken in a stained-glass voice using a code language never heard in the marketplace, dabble in great biblical concepts, but our audience may feel that God belongs to the long ago and far away. We must answer not only the questions our fathers and mothers asked; we must wrestle with the questions our children ask. Men or women who speak effectively for God must first struggle with the questions of their age and then speak to those questions from the eternal truth of God.

A third world in which we must participate is our own particular world. A church has a postal code and stands near Fifth and Main in some town or city. The profound issues of the Bible and the ethical, philosophical questions of our times assume different shapes in rural villages, in middle-class communities, or in the ghettos of crowded cities. Ultimately we do not address everyone; we speak to a particular people and call them by name. The Bible speaks of the gift of pastor-teacher (Eph. 4:11). This implies the two functions should be joined, or else an irrelevant exposition may emerge that reflects negatively on God. As one bewildered churchgoer expressed it, "The trouble is that God is like the minister: we don't see him during the week, and we don't understand him on Sunday." J. M. Reu was on target when he wrote, "Preaching is fundamentally a part of the care of souls, and the care of souls involves a thorough understanding of the congregation."[1] Able shepherds know their flock.

---

1. J. M. Reu, *Homiletics: A Manual of the Theory and Practice of Preaching*, p. 129.

In the following stages, we endeavor to bring the ancient world, the modern world, and our particular world together as we develop the sermon. In doing this we do not make the Bible relevant as though we were drawing an apt illustration from an old story. Modern men and women stand under God in the same position as did their counterparts in the Bible, and they hear the Word of God addressing them now. "Yahweh our God made a covenant with us in Horeb." This affirmation comes from a people hearing the Law a second time decades after it was originally given. Yet they declared through Moses, "Yahweh our God made a covenant with us in Horeb. Not with our fathers did Yahweh make this covenant, but with us, who are all of us here alive this day" (Deut. 5:2–3). The community of faith, looking back at an event that had occurred at a distant time and different place, experienced that history as a present reality. God's word spoken at Sinai continued to speak to this new generation and not only related them to God but also spelled out what God expected in their relation to each other.

To expound the Scriptures so the contemporary God confronts us where we live requires that we study our audience as well as our Bible. It also means that some very nuts-and-bolts questions must be asked and answered to discover how the exegetical idea and its development can expand into a sermon. We relate the Bible to life as we enter the next stage of our study.

Stage 4 Submit your exegetical idea to three developmental questions.

The exegetical idea can lie in our notes like a bowl of soggy cereal. Having stated it, we may wonder if we have anything to preach. How can we bring snap, crackle, and pop to the exegetical idea so that it develops into a sermon that is vital and alive? To answer that practical question, we must be aware of how thought develops.

When we make any declarative statement, we can do only four things with it: we can restate it, explain it, prove it, or apply it. Nothing else. To recognize this simple fact opens the way to understanding the dynamic of thought.

By the use of restatement, an author or speaker merely states an idea "in other words" to clarify it or to impress it on the reader or hearer. Restatement is used in every kind of discourse, but it occupies a major place in the parallelism of Hebrew poetry. "I will sing unto Yahweh as long as I live," the psalmist informs us in Psalm 104:33: "I will sing praise to my God while I have any being" (ASV). He has stated, then restated his idea in different words. The apostle Paul, infuriated by false teachers who substitute legalism for evangelism, uses restatement to emphasize their condemnation. "Though we, or an angel from heaven, should preach unto you any gospel other than that which we preached unto you, let him be damned!" But he restates it: "As we have said before, so say I now again, if any man preaches unto you any gospel other than that which you received, let him be damned" (Gal. 1:8–9).

Jeremiah hammers home his denunciation of Babylon by restating the same thought in at least six different particulars:

> "A sword against the Babylonians!"
>   declares the Lord—
> "against those who live in Babylon
>   and against her officials and wise men!
> A sword against her false prophets!
>   They will become fools.
> A sword against her warriors!
>   They will be filled with terror.
> A sword against her horses and chariots
>   and all the foreigners in her ranks!
>   They will become women.
> A sword against their treasures!
>   They will be plundered.
> A drought on her waters!
>   They will dry up.
> For it is a land of idols,
>   idols that will go mad with terror."
>
>   Jeremiah 50:35–38 NIV

The restatement emphasizes that the Babylonians are in deep trouble!

Restatement takes up a great deal of space in written and especially oral communication, but restatement does not develop thought. It simply says the same thing in other words. To develop a thought, however, we must do one or more of three things. We must explain it, prove it, or apply it. To do this, we can use three developmental questions.[2]

1. WE EXPLAIN IT: "WHAT DOES THIS MEAN?"

The first developmental question centers on explanation: What does this mean? Does this concept, or parts of it, need explanation?

The question, "What does this mean?" can be pointed at different targets. First, it can be directed toward the Bible: "Is the author in the passage before me developing his thought primarily through explanation?" When Paul wrote to his friends at Corinth, he explained how the diversity of gifts granted to its members should work for, and not against, unity in the congregation. He sums up his idea in 1 Corinthians 12:11–12: "But one and the same Spirit works all these things, distributing to each one individually just as He wills. For even as the body is one and yet has many members, and all the members of the body, though they are many, are one body, so also is Christ" (NASB). In the verses surrounding this statement Paul explains the concept either by breaking it down into particulars, such as enumerating spiritual gifts, or by illustrating it through the example of a human body. By that analogy he explains that a church, like a body, consists of many different parts, but each one contributes to the life and benefit of all. A preacher handling this section of the Corinthian letter should be aware that Paul expands his thought primarily through explanation, and that explanation will probably be the major thrust of a sermon from this passage.

When the Apostle Paul wrote to his young associate Titus, he wanted him to appoint elders in Crete. In Titus 1:5–9 Paul ex-

2. H. Grady Davis has developed these questions extensively in relation to the sermon. I am indebted to him for this approach to thinking. It is beyond the scope of Davis's book to apply the questions to the study of Scripture.

plained to Titus what he was to look for in appointing overseers in the churches. He wrote:

> The reason I left you in Crete was that you might straighten out what was left unfinished and appoint elders in every town, as I directed you. An elder must be blameless, the husband of but one wife, a man whose children believe and are not open to the charge of being wild and disobedient. Since an overseer is entrusted with God's work, he must be blameless—not overbearing, not quick-tempered, not given to drunkenness, not violent, not pursuing dishonest gain. Rather he must be hospitable, one who loves what is good, who is self-controlled, upright, holy and disciplined. He must hold firmly to the trustworthy message as it has been taught, so that he can encourage others by sound doctrine and refute those who oppose it. (NIV)

Paul's subject is: "What are the qualifications for a leader in the church?"

His complement is: "The candidate must be 'blameless.'"

Paul states that twice. The apostle explains what "blameless" means in three concrete frameworks: the candidate's family life, his personal life, and his ministry. A sermon based on this passage will do a great deal of explaining of the particulars that Paul lays down. (In addition, you might want to consider other characteristics that might go into a "blameless" leader today.)

Second, the developmental question, "What does this mean?" may also probe the audience. It takes several forms. If I simply stated my exegetical idea, would my audience respond, "What does he mean by that?" Are there elements in the passage that the biblical writer takes for granted that my audience needs explained to them? When Paul advised the Corinthians in 1 Corinthians 8 about meat offered to idols, idolatry and sacrifices were as familiar to his readers as shopping centers are to modern audiences. On the other hand, people today are as bewildered about the practices of idolatry as a Corinthian would be in a supermarket. Therefore, when we talk about "food sacrificed to idols," we must do some explaining. The passage may be misunderstood or, more damaging, misapplied unless our listeners understand the background out of which the problem developed. They must enter into the psychological, emotional, and spiritual tensions posed by eating meat previously offered in sacrifice to heathen gods.

As a case in point, when Paul speaks of a "weak brother," he does not necessarily mean someone who is easily tempted to sin. Instead, he has in mind an over-scrupulous Christian who has not applied theology to experience. The weak Christian does not fully appreciate that "no idol is anything in the world," but is only a creation of superstition. In modern churches, therefore, many over-scrupulous people who consider themselves "strong" would, in Paul's mind, be "weak." In a treatment of this passage, therefore, what Paul took for granted with his readers requires extensive explanation today.

In 1 Corinthians 12:13 the apostle observes: "We were all baptized by one Spirit into one body—whether Jews or Greeks, slave or free—and we were all given the one Spirit to drink" (NIV). Here again Paul assumes that his readers understand the baptizing work of the Holy Spirit. We cannot necessarily assume that our congregation has that knowledge. A reference to "the baptism of the Holy Spirit" now causes some non-charismatic listeners to shift uneasily in their pews and wonder: "What does that mean?" "What do people in my denomination think about it?" "Isn't that an experience important to charismatics, and doesn't it have something to do with speaking in tongues?" In a charismatic congregation, listeners may assume that they know what the baptism of the Holy Spirit is, but wonder what it has to do with Paul's argument. If we were preaching on this passage, therefore, we could not ignore those responses. Instead, we will anticipate them in our preparation, and we may decide to devote some time in the sermon to expand on the baptism of the Holy Spirit even though Paul did not.

Napoleon had three commands for his messengers that apply to any communicator: "Be clear! Be clear! Be clear!" Clarity does not come easily. When we train to be expositors, we will probably spend three or four years in seminary. While that training prepares us to be theologians, it sometimes gets in our way as communicators. Theological jargon, abstract thinking, or schol-

Stage Four

ars' questions become part of the intellectual baggage that hinders preachers from speaking clearly to ordinary men and women. If we entered a hospital, a television studio, a printer's shop, a locker room, or a local garage, and wanted to understand what goes on there, we would persistently ask, "What do you mean?" Experts in other occupations seldom have to make themselves understood to those outside their profession, but preachers are different. No one is an outsider to religion. Everyone must understand what God says. In fact, it is a life-and-death matter. Therefore we must anticipate what our hearers may not know and, by our explanations, help them understand.

The developmental question "What does that mean?" then, deals with both the passage and the people. If you imagine some courageous soul standing up in the middle of your sermon to shout, "Pastor, what exactly do you mean by that?" you will become aware of matters that must be talked about to make yourself clear as your sermon develops.

2. We Prove It: "Is It True?"

Our second developmental question centers on validity. After we understand (or think we understand) what a statement means, we often ask, "Is that true? Can I really believe it?" We demand proof.

An initial response of those of us who take the Scriptures seriously is to ignore this question. We assume that an idea should be accepted as true because it comes from the Bible. That is not necessarily a valid assumption. We may need to gain psychological acceptance in our hearers through reasoning, proofs, or illustrations. Even the inspired writers of the New Testament (all of whom believed that the Old Testament was a God-breathed witness) sometimes established the validity of their statements, not only by quoting the Old Testament but by referring to common life as well.

When Paul wanted to prove to the Corinthian congregation that he had a right to receive financial support for his ministry, for example, he argued not only from the Mosaic Law, but from the experience of farmers, shepherds, and soldiers. In a series of rhetorical questions, he laid out his case:

> Or is it only I and Barnabas who must work for a living? Who serves as a soldier at his own expense? Who plants a vineyard and does not eat of its grapes? Who tends a flock and does not drink of the milk? Do I say this merely from a human point of view? Doesn't the Law say the same thing? For it is written in the Law of Moses: "Do not muzzle an ox while it is treading out the grain." Is it about oxen that God is concerned? Surely he says this for us, doesn't he? Yes, this was written for us, because when the plowman plows and the thresher threshes, they ought to do so in the hope of sharing in the harvest. If we have sown spiritual seed among you, is it too much if we reap a material harvest from you? If others have this right of support from you, shouldn't we have it all the more? (1 Corinthians 9:6–12 NIV)

Paul appealed for proof first to the logic of experience. After all, if soldiers, grape growers, shepherds, and farmers receive wages for their work, why not an apostle or teacher? Then Paul reasoned from an all-embracing principle found in the law against muzzling oxen when they tread out corn. A worker—be it animal or human—should be rewarded for working. In using this developmental question, therefore, we should note how the biblical writers validated what they had to say.

The apostles used every legitimate means available to them to win assent from their audiences. When Peter preached his Pentecost sermon, he reasoned from both experience and Scripture to prove that "God has made Him both Lord and Christ—this Jesus whom you crucified" (Acts 2:36 NASB). Jesus' miracles, the crucifixion, the resurrection, David's tomb, the phenomena of Pentecost: those verifiable events carried the weight of Peter's argument. Joel and David, both honored by the Jewish audience as inspired prophets, were quoted as witnesses to interpret what the people experienced. In both writing and preaching, the apostles adapted themselves to their readers and listeners to establish the validity of their ideas.

When Paul addressed the intellectuals on Mars Hill, he discussed natural theology—the fact of creation and its necessary implications. Although he set forth biblical concepts, the apostle never quoted the Old Testament because the Bible meant nothing to his pagan Greek audience. Rather, he supported his arguments by referring to their idols and poet-philosophers and by drawing deductions from common life. In quoting the Greek poets and philosophers, of course, Paul was not endorsing Athenian philosophy. The Old Testament was the authority for both his major and minor assertions (as the references in the margin of the Nestle Greek text demonstrate). In quoting the pagan sources, Paul merely took advantage of insights consistent with biblical revelation that were more easily accepted by his hearers.[3]

While competence requires that we understand how the biblical writers established validity, it also demands that we wrestle with listeners' questions such as, "Is that true?" and "Can I really believe that?" In a past generation, perhaps, we might have counted on a sense of guilt lying on the fringes of a congregation's thought. Today we can count on an attitude of questioning and doubt. Our educational system and the mass media contribute to this pervasive skepticism. Advertisers have created an audience of doubters who shrug off dogmatic claims and enthusiastic endorsements, no matter who makes them, as nothing more than a pitch from the sponsor.

We do well, therefore, to adopt the attitude that a statement is not true because it is in the Bible; it is in the Bible because it is true. The fact that an assertion is in the pages of a leather-covered book does not necessarily make it valid. Instead, the Bible states reality as it exists in the universe, as God has made it and as He governs it. We would expect, therefore, the affirmations of Scripture to be demonstrated in the world around us. That is not to say that we establish biblical truth by studying sociology, astronomy, or archaeology, but the valid data from these sciences second the truth taught in Scripture.

How does a preacher handle the developmental questions, "Is that true? Do I really believe it?" Imagine that you were to state to a modern congregation the mighty affirmation of Paul, "We

3. N. B. Stonehouse, "The Areopagus Address," in *Paul before the Areopagus and Other New Testament Studies* (Grand Rapids: Eerdmans, 1957), pp. 1–40.

know that in all things God works for the good of those who love him, who have been called according to his purpose" (Rom. 8:28 NIV). Most people greet that statement with raised eyebrows: "Is that true? Can we believe that?" What about the mother who was killed by a hit-and-run driver and who left behind a husband and three children? What about those Christian parents whose four-year-old son has been diagnosed with leukemia? How is that good? What's "good" about a young missionary drowned in the muddy waters of a jungle river before he has witnessed to even one national? To work with this passage and fail to address those perplexing questions is to miss the audience completely.

Donald Grey Barnhouse works with the question of validity while expounding John 14:12: "Greater works than these shall he do; because I go unto my Father" (KJV). He used an analogy to establish the truth of his explanation:

Aboard a United States submarine in enemy waters of the Pacific, a sailor was stricken with acute appendicitis. The nearest surgeon was thousands of miles away. Pharmacist Mate Wheller Lipes watched the seaman's temperature rise to 106 degrees. His only hope was an operation. Said Lipes: "I have watched doctors do it. I think I could. What do you say?" The sailor consented. In the wardroom, about the size of a Pullman drawing room, the patient was stretched out on a table beneath a floodlight. The mate and assisting officers, dressed in reversed pajama tops, masked their faces with gauze. The crew stood by the diving planes to keep the ship steady: the cook boiled water for sterilizing. A tea strainer served as an antiseptic cone. A broken-handled scalpel was the operating instrument. Alcohol drained from the torpedoes was the antiseptic. Bent tablespoons served to keep the muscles open. After cutting through the layers of muscle, the mate took twenty minutes to find the appendix. Two hours and a half later, the last catgut stitch was sewed, just as the last drop of ether gave out. Thirteen days later the patient was back at work.

Admittedly this was a much more magnificent feat than if it had been performed by trained surgeons in a fully equipped operating room of a modern hospital. Study this analogy and you will know the real meaning of Christ's words. "Greater works than these shall he do; because I go unto my Father." For Christ, perfect God, to work directly on a lost soul to quicken and bring out of death and into life is great, but for Him to do the same thing through us is a greater work.[4]

Cynddylan Jones works to win belief with a single sentence: "You might as well try to cross the Atlantic in a paper boat," he declares, "as to get to heaven by your own good works."

C. S. Lewis comes at validity by identifying himself with a question that thoughtful people have about the gospel:

> Here is another thing that used to puzzle me. Is it not frightfully unfair that this new life should be confined to people who have heard of Christ and been able to believe in Him? But the truth is God has not told us what His arrangements about the other people are. We do know that no man can be saved except through Christ; we do not know that only those who know about Him can be saved through Him. But in the meantime, if you worried about the people outside, the most unreasonable thing you can do is to remain outside yourself. Christians are Christ's body, the organism through which He works. Every addition to that body enables Him to do more. If you want to help those outside, you must add your own little cell to the body of Christ who alone can help them. Cutting off a man's fingers would be an odd way of getting him to do more work.[5]

Whether you fully agree with Lewis or not, he raises a classic question, deals with it, and turns it back upon the questioner.

J. Wallace Hamilton, preaching on the providence of God, understands the serious questions that are raised when we are told that we live by the providence of God every moment of our lives. He quotes an anonymous poet as he begins to deal with the doubts:

> "Oh, where is the sea" the fishes cried,
> As they swam the Atlantic waters through;

4. Donald Grey Barnhouse, *Let Me Illustrate: Stories, Anecdotes, Illustrations* (Old Tappan, N.J.: Revell, 1967), pp. 358–59.

5. C. S. Lewis, *Mere Christianity* (New York: Macmillan, 1952), p. 50.

Stage Four

"We've heard of the sea and the ocean tide
And we long to gaze on its waters blue."

All around us are little fishes looking for the sea; people living, moving, having their being in an ocean of God's providence, but who can't see the ocean for the water. Maybe it's because we call it by another name. The ancient Hebrews from whom the Bible came were a religious people. They thought in religious patterns, they spoke in religious phrases, they saw in every event the direct activity of God. If it rained, it was God who sent the rain. When crops were good, it was God who yielded the increase. But that is not our language, nor the pattern of our thought. We think in terms of law—chemical, natural law. When it rains we know it is the natural condensation of vapor. When crops are good we credit it to the fertilizer. An amazing thing has happened in our way of thinking. In a world that could not for one moment exist without the activity of God, we have conditioned our minds to a way of thinking that leaves no room for him. So many of our wants are provided by what seem natural and impersonal forces that we have lost sight of the great Provider in the midst of providence. Some of us who were brought up in the country and then later moved to the city remember how easy it was to get out of the habit of returning thanks at the table, partly because the food on it came not directly from the earth but from the grocery store. A physician in New York City said, "If you ask a child where milk comes from, he won't think of saying "From a cow." He will say "From a container."[6]

Stage Four

Merely to ask, "Is that true? Do I and my hearers believe that?" does not produce instant answers. But failing to contend with those basic questions means we will speak only to those who are already committed. Worse, because we have not been willing to live for a time on the sloping back of a question mark, we may become hucksters for a message that we do not believe ourselves. A congregation has the right to expect that we are at least aware of the problems before we offer solutions. Work your way through the ideas in the exegetical outline and deal honestly

6. J. Wallace Hamilton, *Who Goes There? What and Where Is God?* (Westwood, N.J.: Revell, 1958), p. 52.

with the question, "Would my audience accept that statement as true? If not, why not?" Write down the specific questions that come and, if possible, the direction of some of the answers. Before long you will discover much that you and your hearers have to think about as the sermon develops.

3. WE APPLY IT: "WHAT DIFFERENCE DOES IT MAKE?"

The third developmental question relates to application. While it is essential that you explain the truth of a passage, your task is not finished until you relate that passage to the experience of your hearers. Ultimately the man or woman in the pew hopes that you will answer the questions, "So what? What difference does it make?" All Christians have a responsibility to ask these questions because they are called to live under God in the light of biblical revelation.

Mortimer J. Adler classifies books as either theoretical or practical. A theoretical book may be understood and then put away on the shelf. A practical book, however, must not only be read, it must also be used. Taken in this way, the Bible is an intensely practical book because it was written not only to be understood, but to be obeyed.

Homileticians have not given accurate application the attention it deserves. To my knowledge, no book has been published that is devoted exclusively, or even primarily, to the knotty problems raised by application.[7] As a result many church members, having listened to orthodox sermons all their lives, may be practicing heretics. Our creeds affirm the central doctrines of the faith and remind us what Christians should believe, but they do not tell us how belief in these doctrines should make us behave. That is part of the expositor's responsibility, and you must give it diligent attention.

---

7. The new hermeneutic, to its credit, has embraced application as well as exegesis, but in the effort to apply the Bible creatively, it sometimes seems less concerned with understanding Scripture correctly.

Basic to perceptive application is accurate exegesis. We cannot decide what a passage means to us unless first we have determined what the passage meant when the Bible was written. To do this we must sit down before the biblical writer and try to understand what he wanted to convey to his original readers. Only after we comprehend what he meant in his own terms and to his own times can we clarify what difference that should make in life today.

In order to apply a passage accurately, we must define the situation into which the revelation was originally given and then decide what a modern man or woman shares, or does not share, with the original readers. The closer the relationship between people now and people then, the more direct the application. James wrote to Jewish Christians scattered across the ancient world and facing hard situations, "My dear brothers, take note of this: Everyone should be quick to listen, slow to speak and slow to become angry, for man's anger does not bring about the righteous life that God desires" (James 1:19–20 NIV). That counsel applies to believers in every age because all Christians stand in identical relationship to God and His Word when they face trials.

When the correspondence between the twenty-first century and the biblical passage is less direct, however, accurate application becomes more difficult. An expositor must give special attention not only to what modern men and women have in common with those who received the original revelation but also to the differences between them. For instance, Paul's many exhortations to slaves had direct application to Christian slaves in the first century and those throughout history. Many of the principles touched on in the master-slave relationship can also govern employer-employee relationships today, but to ignore the fact that modern employees are not slaves to their employers would lead to gross misapplication of these passages. For example, denouncing membership in a labor union because slaves are to "obey" their "masters" (Eph. 6:5) would be to ignore completely the distinction between employees and slaves.

The problems multiply when we apply texts from the Old Testament to contemporary audiences. Indeed, misapplication of the Old Testament has had an embarrassing history. One unsat-

Stage Four

isfying approach lies in using these passages like a sanctified Rorschach test. Interpreters allegorized Old Testament stories to find in them hidden meanings that were not buried in the text, but in their own minds.

Origen, for example, allegorized the account of the battle for Jericho (Josh. 6). He maintained that Joshua stood for Jesus, and the city of Jericho represented the world. The seven priests who carried trumpets around the city represented Matthew, Mark, Luke, John, James, Jude, and Peter. Rahab, the harlot, stood for the Church, which is made up of sinners; and the scarlet cord that she displayed to deliver herself and her household was the blood of Christ.[8] Commentators who use allegory deserve high marks for creativity but low marks for approaching the biblical account as literature.

Another inadequate method of handling the Old Testament uses it only as an example or illustration of New Testament doctrine. Here the authority for what is preached comes neither from the theology of the Old Testament nor from the intent of the Old Testament writer, but entirely from the reader's theology read back into the passage. Should those who do this be challenged about their interpretation or application, they appeal not to the passage before them, but to some passage in the New Testament or to a theology that they assume they share with their audience.

How then can we proceed as we answer the third developmental question, "So what? What difference does it make?" Application must come from the theological purpose of the biblical writer. John Bright states the case for determining the author's intent: ". . . the preacher needs to understand not only what the text says, but also those concerns that caused it to be said, and said as it was. His exegetical labors are, therefore, not complete until he has grasped the text's theological intention. Until he has done this he cannot interpret the text, and may egregiously misinterpret it by attributing to its words an intention quite other than that of their author."[9]

---

8. Arthur Wainwright, *Beyond Biblical Criticism: Encountering Jesus in Scripture* (London: SPCK, 1982), p. 87.

9. John Bright, *The Authority of the Old Testament* (Nashville: Abingdon, 1967; reprint, Grand Rapids: Baker, 1975), pp. 171–72.

We cannot understand or apply an individual passage, whether in the Old Testament or in the New, until we have studied its context. For instance, plunging into an analysis of a paragraph or chapter of Ecclesiastes without first gaining an appreciation for the thrust of the entire book might lead to many heretical ideas and devastating applications for people today. Only after mastering the larger passage do we find the clues for understanding what the smaller texts mean and why they were written.

Here are some questions that help us discover the author's theological purpose:

1. *Are there in the text any indications of purpose, editorial comments, or interpretive statements made about events?* In the Book of Ruth, for example, the material in chapter 4:11–21 provides a happy ending to a story with a gloomy beginning, and it affirms God's gracious direction in the lives of the characters involved. Ruth demonstrates the providence of God. The theme of God's loving guidance, brought into focus in the conclusion, is implied throughout the book—especially in the seven prayers of blessing and in the common, ordinary way each prayer is answered. God's working is woven into the tapestry of everyday events so skillfully that at first reading we may not see Him at work at all. Only on reflection do we become aware that God was continuously acting to meet the needs and hopes of ordinary people.[10] What you could not legitimately preach from Ruth is a sermon on "How to Deal with a Difficult In-Law." Although Ruth reflects tensions between a mother-in-law and her daughter-in-law, the book was not written to solve in-law problems. A sermon on this subject using Ruth might offer some practical advice about how to handle family conflicts, but it would have no Scriptural authority. It ignores completely what the author intended. Worse, it leads listeners to believe that

Stage Four

---

10. For a splendid development of this theme and its application, see Ronald M. Hals, *The Theology of the Book of Ruth* (Philadelphia: Fortress, 1969).

any advice sprinkled with Bible verses can be considered what God says on the matter.[11]

2. *Are there any theological judgments made in the text?* Comments such as "In those days Israel had no king; everyone did as he saw fit" (NIV), made twice in the book of Judges (17:6; 21:25), point to why these sordid accounts are recorded as part of Israel's history. The narrative of David's sin with Bathsheba and his murder of Uriah flows from the pen of the historian in a matter-of-fact way until we reach the statement in 2 Samuel 11:27, "But the thing David had done displeased the Lord" (NIV). That single sentence is the theological statement that puts into perspective the event and what follows in 2 Samuel.

3. Narrative passages of the Bible offer special difficulties to the interpreter. In addition to the questions normally raised, we should ask, *Is this story given as an example or warning? If so, in exactly what way? Is this incident a norm or an exception? What limitations should be placed on it?* For example, in the story of Rahab (Josh. 2:1–7) you cannot derive any lessons about the morality of deception, but in light of several New Testament passages (Heb. 11:31, James 2:25), you can conclude that Rahab was a woman with a vibrant faith.

4. *What message was intended for those to whom the revelation was originally given and also for subsequent generations the writer knew would read it?*

5. *Why would the Holy Spirit have included this account in Scripture?* If it were not in the Bible, would anything be lost?

There are other questions we must ask in order to apply God's Word to a contemporary audience living in a situation different from that of the people to whom the revelation was originally given.

11. See also Robert L. Hubbard Jr., *The Book of Ruth,* New International Commentary on the Old Testament (Grand Rapids: Eerdmans, 1988).

1. *What was the setting in which God's Word first came? What traits do modern men and women share in common with that original audience?* For example, Deuteronomy was spoken by Moses to a new generation on the far side of the Jordan River. Members of his audience believed in Yahweh and were part of a theocracy established by God's covenant. God had entered into a treaty with them that spelled out in detail the rewards and punishments for their obedience or disobedience. All of them had come out of the wilderness with Moses, and they looked forward to entering the land God had promised to Abraham.

   Christians today cannot be directly identified with that nation of Israel. The church is neither a theocracy nor a nation. We are, however, believers in Yahweh, and we are the people of God, chosen by His grace to be witnesses to the world. In addition, like them, we have revelation from God that He expects us to obey.

2. *How can we identify with biblical men and women as they heard God's Word and responded—or failed to respond in their situation?* While we cannot identify with the Israelites in actually entering the land of Canaan, or with David reigning as a king in Jerusalem, or with the life-situation of a Hebrew under the law, we do share common humanity with these men and women. We can identify with their intellectual, emotional, psychological, and spiritual reactions to God and to others around them.

   We would do well to remember J. Daniel Baumann's observation: "We are very much like the people of the ancient world. It is only in some superficial thoughts, rational beliefs, and mental moods that we are different. In all of the basic heart realities we are the same. We stand before God exactly as people in every age have stood before Him. We have all experienced David's guilt, the doubting of Thomas, Peter's denial, the falling away of Demas, perhaps even the kiss of the betrayer Judas. We are linked across the centuries by the realities and ambiguities of the human soul."[12] In all the biblical accounts, God confronts men and women, and we may enter into the responses people make to God and to others as individuals, in a group, or both. That same God whose person and character never changes addresses us today in our situations, and the principles and dynamics involved in these encounters remain very much the same throughout history.

3. *What further insights have we acquired about God's dealings with His people through additional revelation?* Mystery writers often work into the first chapter of their novel incidents that appear irrelevant or perplexing. The significance of those events becomes obvious in later chapters. Because the Bible stands entire and complete, no passage should be interpreted or applied in isolation from all that God has spoken. Each text should be interpreted within the book in which it appears. But each of the books of the Bible makes up a part of the entire revelation. Sometimes what we may overlook in the beginning of the Scriptures becomes a clue to a fuller revelation.

4. *When I understand an eternal truth or guiding principle, what specific, practical applications does this have for me and my congregation? What ideas, feelings, attitudes, or actions should it affect? Do I myself live in obedience to this truth? Do I intend to? What obstacles keep my audience from responding as they should? What suggestions might help them respond as God wants them to respond?*

Ordinarily you begin your study with a single passage of Scripture, and your application comes directly or by necessary implication from that passage. If you begin with a specific need in your congregation and turn to the Bible for solutions, then you must decide first what passages address the questions being raised. Through your exegesis of those separate passages, then, you explore the subject. When the Bible speaks directly to those ques-

12. J. Daniel Baumann, *An Introduction to Contemporary Preaching*, p. 100.

tions in a variety of texts, application and authority still come directly from Scripture.

Application becomes more complex, however, when we must deal with problems biblical writers never encountered. Because Jesus Christ stands as Lord over history, Christians must respond to current ethical and political concerns from a divine perspective. We assume that the Holy Spirit has a will for such matters as abortion, test-tube babies, protecting the environment, hunger in the world, the use of technology, or government welfare programs. But the Bible cannot and does not speak directly to all moral or political situations, and as a result, how we believe, vote, or act is not mandated directly by the Scriptures. Whether we can say "Thus saith the Lord" about particular issues not dealt with in the Bible depends on our analysis of the issues and our application of theological principles. How we state the question and what parts of the issue we emphasize may shape our conclusion. Several questions help us test the accuracy of our application:

1. Have I correctly understood the facts and properly formulated the questions involved in the issue? Can those questions be stated another way so that other issues emerge? Would those who disagree with me state the issue another way?
2. Have I determined all the theological principles that must be considered? Do I give the same weight to each principle? Are there other principles that I have chosen to ignore?
3. Is the theology I espouse truly biblical, derived from disciplined exegesis and accurate interpretation of biblical passages? Proof-texting poses a special danger here. This practice finds support for a doctrine or ethical position in passages ripped from their context or interpreted without reference to the author's purpose, or without looking at other passages that may limit the application.

Stage Four

In the forming of these moral and political judgments, Alexander Miller offers helpful insight: "A valid Christian decision is compounded always of both *faith and facts*. It is likely to be valid in the degree to which the faith is rightly apprehended and the facts are rightly measured."[13] Because our analysis of facts and our interpretation of the faith may differ, Christians disagree on ethical and political issues. Yet unless we struggle with the facts in the light of our faith, no decisions we make can legitimately be called *Christian*.

God reveals Himself in the Scriptures. The Bible, therefore, isn't a textbook about ethics or a manual on how to solve personal problems. The Bible is a book about God. When you study a biblical text, therefore, you should ask, "What is the vision of God in this passage?" God is always there. Look for Him. At different times He is the Creator, a good Father, the Redeemer, a rejected Lover, a Husband, a King, a Savior, a Warrior, a Judge, a Reaper, a vineyard Keeper, a banquet Host, a Fire, a Hen protecting her chicks, and so on.

As you study, then, there are at least four questions you want to ask of a passage.

- First, what is the vision of God in this particular text?
- Second, where precisely do I find that in the passage? (The vision of God is always in the specific words and the life situation of the writer or the readers.)
- Third, what is the function of this vision of God? What implications for belief or behavior did the author draw from the image?
- Fourth, what is the significance of that picture of God for me and for others?[14]

Not only is it important to look for the vision of God in a passage, but you will also want to look at the human factor. How should people in the biblical text have responded to this vision of God? How *did* they respond? Should this vision of God have made any practical difference in their lives? This human factor is the condition that men and women today have in common with

13. Alexander Miller, *The Renewal of Man: A Twentieth-Century Essay on Justification by Faith* (Garden City, N.Y.: Doubleday, 1955), p. 94.

14. To see this spelled out in some detail, look at H. Edward Everding Jr. and Dana W. Wilbanks, *Decision Making and the Bible* (Valley Forge, Pa.: Judson, 1975), chapter 5.

Stage Four

the characters in the Bible. The human factor may show up in sins such as rebellion, unbelief, adultery, greed, laziness, selfishness, or gossip. It may also show up in people puzzling about the human condition as a result of sickness, grief, anxiety, doubt, trials, or the sense that God has misplaced their names and addresses. It is this human factor that usually prompted the prophets and apostles to speak or write what they did.[15]

To apply a passage, therefore, you need to see what your passage reveals about God and the way people responded and lived before God. Look for those same factors in contemporary life. How does the condition of people today reflect the sins, fears, hopes, frustrations, anxieties, and confusion of women and men centuries ago? What vision of God do they need? How do they respond or not respond to that vision? In this way, you can move with integrity from the biblical text to the modern situation.[16]

Think about specific ways this biblical truth about God and people would actually work out in experience. To do that, ask yourself questions like:

- Where do the dynamics of the biblical situation show up today?
- So what? What real difference does this truth about God make to me or to others? What difference should it make? What difference could it make? Why doesn't it make a difference?
- Can I picture for my listeners in specific terms how this vision of God might be one they need in a particular situation? Would there ever be an occasion when someone might come to me with a problem or need and I would point them to this passage and this truth? Listeners feel that a sermon is relevant when they can say, "I can *see* how that would apply to my life."

15. Bryan Chapell, in *Christ-Centered Preaching*, refers to this as the "Fallen Condition Factor" (FCF) on pages 40–44.

16. To pursue this pattern further, read Harold Freeman, *Variety in Biblical Preaching*, pp. 41ff. He offers another way to approach application. You may also want to look at my article on "The Heresy of Application" in *Leadership* (fall 1997): 20–27.

Stage Four

To be effective, sermons must relate biblical truth to life. The most effective sermons are those that do this in a specific, not a general, way. If you do not apply the Scriptures to people's life experience, you cannot expect that they will do it. James warned us about the danger of "hearing the Word" but not acting on it. Listeners are deceived if they simply know God's Word but do not practice it. As preachers, we dare not contribute to that delusion. Our hearers need both truth to believe and specific, life-shaping ways to apply it.

These three developmental questions, then, prod our thinking and help us decide what must be said about our passage. Take these questions and direct them toward the details of your text, and then direct them toward your audience. Write down what must be said to answer the questions. You will soon know whether or not you have a sermon and what kind of study you will have to do to make your sermon effective.

Note that the questions build on each other. Only when we think we understand a statement do we question its validity. And only when we understand and believe a statement will it make a positive difference in our lives. While you may deal with all three questions in the development of your sermon, one of the three predominates and determines the form your message will take. All of this probing leads you toward your homiletical idea, which occupies you in the next stage of development.

Stage Four

New Concepts

Restatement
Three developmental questions

Definitions

Three developmental questions—

1. What does this mean? Explores explanation.
2. Is it true? Do I believe it? Explores validity.
3. So what? What difference does it make? Explores implications and applications.

Restatement—the statement of an idea in different words to clarify it or to impress it upon the audience.

Exercises

Determine the subject and complement in the following exercises. In addition indicate what developmental question you think each author answers.

1. "The reason you can't teach an old dog new tricks is not that he is incapable of learning them. It is that he is quite content with his mastery of the old tricks, and thinks that learning new tricks is strictly for puppies. Besides, he is busy paying off the mortgage on the dog house." (John W. Gardner)

   Subject: _____

   Complement: _____

   Developmental question being addressed: _____

   _____

2. "The powerful voice of God warns of judgment, and the same voice expresses His compassion for those who come back to Him in His given way. We are to listen with the same intensity of awe we feel when we observe the power of wa-

ter. His spoken truth is not for us to judge or edit; we are to
listen, absorb, understand, and bow." (Edith Schaeffer)

Subject: _____

Complement: _____

Developmental question being addressed: _____

_____

3. "The best thing you can do for your golf this winter is look
in a mirror. A full-length mirror is a valuable learning aid.
With it you can make valuable improvement, particularly in
your set-up position and putting." *(New York Times)*

Subject: _____

Complement: _____

Developmental question being addressed: _____

_____ _____

4. "Let no debt remain outstanding, except the continuing
debt to love one another, for he who loves his fellow man
has fulfilled the law. The commandments, 'Do not commit
adultery,' 'Do not murder,' 'Do not steal,' 'Do not covet' and
whatever other commandments there may be, are summed
up in this one rule: 'Love your neighbor as yourself.' Love
does no harm to its neighbor. Therefore love is the fulfillment of the law." (Romans 13:8–10)

Subject: _____

Complement: _____

Developmental question being addressed: _____

_____

5. A Chinese boy who wanted to learn about jade went to study
with a talented old teacher. This gentleman put a piece of the
stone into the youth's hand and told him to hold it tight. Then

he began to talk of philosophy, men, women, the sun and almost everything under it. After an hour he took back the stone and sent the boy home. The procedure was repeated for weeks. The boy became frustrated—when would he be told about jade?—but he was too polite to interrupt his venerable teacher. Then one day when the old man put a stone into his hands, the boy cried out instantly, "That's not jade!"

Subject: _____

Complement: _____

Developmental question being addressed: _____

_____

6. "Rudolph Fellner reminds his classes at Carnegie-Mellon University that 'melody exists only in your memory, for at any given moment you are hearing only one note of the tune.' Music is a cumulative art. It is a change of sounds through time, each sound taking its meaning from those that have gone before. It is not the art for amnesiacs." (William Mayer)

Subject: _____

Complement: _____

Developmental question being addressed: _____

_____

7. I shall pass through this life but once.
   Any good, therefore, that I can do
   Or any kindness I can show to any fellow creature,
   Let me do it now.
   Let me not defer or neglect it,
   For I shall not pass this way again.

Subject: _____

Complement: _____

Developmental question being addressed: _____

_____

8. "Work today has lost many traditional characteristics; so has play. Play has increasingly been transformed into organized sports, and sports in turn increasingly resemble work in the arduous practice and preparation, in the intense involvement of coaches and athletes (in the spirit of work), and in actual economic productivity. In a final paradox only those sports which began as work—that is, hunting and fishing— are now dominated by the spirit of play." *(Sport and Society)*

Subject: _____

Complement: _____

Developmental question being addressed: _____

_____

9. The law can prompt us to sin. I am told that several years ago a high-rise hotel was built in Galveston, Texas, overlooking the Gulf of Mexico. In fact, they sank pilings into the gulf and built the structure out over the water. When the hotel was about to have its grand opening, someone thought, "What if people decide to fish out the hotel windows?" So they placed signs in the hotel rooms, "No fishing out the hotel windows." Many people ignored the signs, however, and it created a difficult problem. Lines got snarled. People in the dining room saw fish flapping against the picture windows. The manager of the hotel solved it all by taking down those little signs. No one checks into a hotel room thinking about fishing out of the windows. The law, although well-intentioned, created the problem.

Subject: _____

Complement: _____

Developmental question being addressed: _____

_____

(Answers are in appendix 1.)

five

THE ARROW
and the Target

Let's take a moment to review. In the first two stages of your preparation, you study the text to determine the exegetical idea and its development. You want to state the subject and the complement of what the biblical writer wrote to his readers. Also make a rough outline, or sketch, of the passage. How did the author develop his idea?

101

Having done that, you still face the question, "Do I have anything to preach?" While every good sermon is the development of
a central idea, not every idea in the biblical text can be turned into
a sermon. In the next stage, therefore, you submit your exegetical
idea and its development to the three developmental questions:

- What does this mean?
- Is this true? Do I believe it?
- So what? What difference does this make?

These three questions deal with the meaning, validity, and implications of any idea. The questions should be addressed not only
to the main idea but to the supporting ideas and the details of the
passage as well. This helps you decide what kind of supporting materials you will need to communicate the message of your text.

You also keep your audience in mind as you answer these
three questions:

"What does this mean?" What has to be explained so that my listeners will understand the passage?

- Does the biblical writer explain his statements or define his
  terms? Does he assume that the original readers understood
  him and needed no explanation?
- Are there concepts, terms, or connections that modern listeners might not understand that you need to explain to
  them?

"Is this true? Do I really believe it?" What needs to be proved?

- Is the author arguing, proving, or defending at length some
  concept that your hearers would probably accept—for example, that Jesus was human, or that Christians don't have
  to be circumcised?
- Is the author arguing, proving, or defending a concept that
  your listeners may not readily accept, and therefore they

need to understand the argument of the passage—for instance, that slaves were to be obedient to their masters?

- Is the author assuming the validity of an idea that your listeners may not accept right away? Do they need to be convinced that what the passage asserts is actually the case—for instance, that Jesus is the only way to God, or that demons actually exist?

"So what? What difference does it make?" How should this concept be applied?

- Is the biblical writer applying his idea? Where does he develop it? Exhortations in the Scriptures grow out of the context. Some sermons resemble cut flowers: the admonition of the author is cut off from the truth that produced it. The imperatives are always connected to the indicative. The effect should be traced to its cause.
- Is the author presenting an idea that he doesn't apply directly but will apply later in his letter? Where does he do that? How do you apply this truth to your listeners now?
- Does the biblical writer assume that the reader will see the application of an assertion? The writers of the gospels often assume that the readers will see the implication of a parable or a miracle. In narrative literature especially, ask yourself, "Why did the author include this incident?"

As you work through these questions, jot down what you must explain, prove, or apply to your hearers. You will soon know whether you have anything to preach and what research you must do. You will see the general direction your sermon must go and what you must deal with in your sermon.

Stage 5 In light of the audience's knowledge and experience, think through your exegetical idea and state it in the most exact, memorable sentence possible.

In stage five, state the essence of your exegetical idea in a sentence that communicates to your listeners. This sentence is your

Stage Five

homiletical idea. Remember that you are not lecturing to people about the Bible. You are talking to people about themselves from the Bible. This statement, therefore, should be in fresh, vital, contemporary language.

Advertisers know that while we do not remember abstractions, we do remember slogans. Although advertising slogans are usually "much ado about nothing," we should not underestimate the power of an idea well stated. People are more likely to think God's thoughts after Him, and to live and love and choose on the basis of those thoughts, when they are couched in memorable sentences.

Some statements of the homiletical idea may be identical to the statement of the exegetical idea. That is the case when you are dealing with universal principles that apply to anyone at any time: "Do not commit adultery," "Do not steal," or "Love your neighbor as you love yourself" need no translation into the twenty-first century. They are already there. "A soft answer turns away wrath, but a grievous word stirs up anger" is timeless. Habakkuk declared, "The righteous [person] shall live by his faith" (Hb. 2:4 ASV). This foundational idea of Scripture doesn't need to be made contemporary. It needs only to be explained and applied.

Other exegetical ideas, however, are turned into homiletical ideas when you make them more up-to-date or personal. The exegetical idea of 1 Thessalonians 1:2–10 might be, "Paul thanked God for the Thessalonians because through the apostle's ministry, God had brought them to himself and made a noticeable difference in their lives." The preaching idea should be more direct and personal: "Thank God regularly for the Christians you know because of what God has done for them and is doing through them."

An exegetical statement of 1 Timothy 4:12–16 might be, "Paul exhorted young Timothy to win respect by being an example to others both in his personal life and in his public ministry of the Scriptures." Were this passage the basis of a sermon to seminary students, the idea might be stated: "Win respect for yourself both by the way you live and the way you teach."

Your homiletical statement can be more contemporary and less tied to the words of the text. Don Sunukjian preached a sermon on Exodus 13:17–18:

> Now it came about when Pharaoh had let the people go, that God did not lead them by the way of the land of the Philistines, even though it was near; for God said, 'Lest the people change their minds when they see war, and they return to Egypt.' Hence God led the people around by way of the wilderness to the Red Sea; and the sons of Israel went up in martial array from the land of Egypt. (NASB)

Sunukjian's preaching idea was, "The shortest distance between two points may be a zigzag." That was true to the text, and it is also true to life.

When James Rose expounded Romans 12:1–17, his homiletical idea was, "When the effect of the gospel is all-important in the church, the force of the gospel is unstoppable in the world."

In preaching Romans 2:1–19, you might have as your central concept, "If you use the law as your ladder to heaven, you will be left standing in hell."

The exegetical statement of Romans 6:1–14 might be, "Through their union with Jesus Christ in his death and resurrection, Christians have died to the rule of sin and are alive to holiness." Here's a more striking statement for that idea: "You are not the person you used to be; therefore, don't handle life as you used to handle it."

The central lesson from the parable of the Good Samaritan (Luke 10:25–37) might be, "Your neighbor is anyone whose need you see, whose need you are in a position to meet."

As you can see, the homiletical idea is simply the biblical truth applied to life.

Here are some general suggestions for framing a homiletical idea:

- State the idea as simply and as memorably as possible. Make each word count. State it for the ear. Listeners should not have to work to remember it.

- State the idea in concrete and familiar words. Study ads in magazines for slogans you remember. If you were given one sentence in which to communicate your idea to someone who didn't know religious jargon and who couldn't write it down, how would you say it?

- State the idea so that it focuses on response. How do you want your listeners to respond? Instead of "You can rejoice in trials because they lead to maturity," try "Rejoice when hard times come." If you know what your listeners should do, tell them.

- State the idea so that your listeners sense you are talking to them about them.

THE POWER OF PURPOSE

The noted preacher R. W. Dale was evidently a man who was as secure as the Rock of Gibraltar. Every Saturday evening he delivered his sermon to his wife. One day, after he had gone through this exercise, his wife asked, "Tell me, why are you preaching that sermon?"

That obvious question faces all of us as we prepare, and it receives many inadequate answers. For example, "When 11:25 comes on Sunday morning, I'll be expected to say something religious." Or "Last week I covered Genesis 21, so this week I'll preach on Genesis 22." Sometimes our response to the question, "Why are you preaching that sermon?" is as clear as a thick fog: "I'm preaching this sermon because I want to give the people a challenge." Such answers, usually implied rather than stated, produce sermons that resemble a dropped lemon meringue pie— they splatter over everything, but hit nothing very hard. They lack a definite purpose!

No matter how brilliant or biblical a sermon is, without a definite purpose it is not worth preaching. We have no adequate idea of why we are speaking. Imagine asking a hockey coach, "What is the purpose of your hockey team?" He had better know the answer. All kinds of activities take place on the ice—skating, stick handling, checking, passing—but the purpose of a hockey team must be to outscore the opponent. A team that does not keep that firmly in mind plays only for exercise. Why preach this sermon? We do an assortment of things when we face our congregation. We explain, illustrate, exhort, exegete, and gesture, to list a few. But we are to be pitied if we fail to understand that this particular sermon should change lives in some specific way. A. W. Tozer speaks a perceptive word to all of us:

> There is scarcely anything so dull and meaningless as Bible doctrine taught for its own sake. Truth divorced from life is not truth in its Biblical sense, but something else and something less. . . . No man is better for knowing that God in the beginning created the heaven and the earth. The devil knows that, and so did Ahab and Judas Iscariot. No man is better for knowing that God so loved the world of men that He gave His only begotten Son to die for their redemption. In hell there are millions who know that. Theological truth is useless until it is obeyed. The purpose behind all doctrine is to secure moral action.[1]

The purpose behind each individual sermon is to secure some moral action. We need to know what that action is.

Stage 6   Determine the purpose for this sermon.

The purpose states what you expect to happen in your hearers as a result of preaching your sermon. George Sweazey maintains that a purpose distinguishes a sermon from an essay: "An essay looks at ideas, but a sermon looks at people."[2] A purpose differs from the sermon idea, therefore, in the same way that a target differs from the arrow; as taking a trip differs from studying a map; as baking a pie differs from reading a recipe. Whereas the idea states the truth, the purpose defines what that truth should accomplish. Henry Ward Beecher appreciated the importance of purpose when he declared: "A sermon is not like a

1. A. W. Tozer, *Of God and Men* (Harrisburg, Pa.: Christian Publications, 1960), pp. 26–27.
2. George E. Sweazey, *Preaching the Good News* (Englewood Cliffs, N.J.: Prentice-Hall, 1976).

Chinese firecracker to be fired off for the noise it makes. It is a hunter's gun, and at every discharge he should look to see his game fall." That presupposes, of course, that the hunter knows what he is hunting.

How then do you determine the purpose of your sermon? You do so by discovering the purpose behind the passage you are preaching. As part of your exegesis, you should ask, "Why did the author write this? What effect did he expect it to have on his readers?" No biblical writer took up his pen to jot down "a few appropriate remarks" on a religious subject. Each one wrote to affect lives. For instance, when Paul wrote to Timothy, he did it "so that you may know how one ought to conduct himself in the household of God, which is the church of the living God, the pillar and support of the truth" (1 Tim. 3:15 NASB).

Jude changed purposes for his letter after he sat down to write. "While I was making every effort to write you about our common salvation," he confessed, "I felt the necessity to write to you appealing that you contend earnestly for the faith which was once for all delivered to the saints" (Jude 3 NASB). John designed his account of Jesus' life to win belief in Jesus as "the Christ, the Son of God" and to secure in believers "life through his name" (John 20:31 KJV). Whole books, as well as sections within books, were written to make something happen in the thinking and the actions of the readers. An expository sermon, therefore, finds its purpose in line with the biblical purposes. You must first figure out why a particular passage was included in the Bible, and with this in mind decide what God desires to accomplish through your sermon in your hearers today.

The inspired Scriptures were given so that we could be "adequate, equipped for every good work" (2 Tim. 3:16–17 NASB). It follows from this that you should be able to put into words what beliefs, attitudes, or values should change or be confirmed, or what quality of life or what good works should result from the preaching and hearing of your sermon. You accomplish that purpose, Paul told Timothy, through (1) teaching a doctrine, (2) refuting some error in belief or action, (3) correcting what is wrong, and (4) instructing people on the proper handling of life.

Educators realize that an effective statement of purpose goes beyond procedure and describes the observable behavior that should come as a result of teaching. A purpose statement not only describes our destination and the route we will follow to get there, but, if possible, tells how we can know if we have arrived. If we are not clear about where we are going, we will probably land someplace else.[3]

Roy B. Zuck has drawn up a list of verbs valuable for stating course objectives. These verbs are useful for dealing with the purpose of giving knowledge and insight (the cognitive domain) and changing attitudes and actions (the affective domain). This list is reproduced in table 1.

While preaching differs significantly from lecturing, stating the purpose of a sermon as though it were an instructional objective makes the sermon more direct and effective. Here are some purposes stated in measurable terms:

- The listener should understand justification by faith and be able to write out a simple definition of the doctrine. (Whether the hearers actually write out the definition or not, you will be much more specific if you preach as though they will.)
- A listener should be able to list the spiritual gifts and determine which gifts he or she has been given.
- A listener should be able to write down the name of at least one non-Christian and should resolve to pray for that individual each day for the next two weeks. (If listeners do something for two weeks, they have a better chance of doing it for several months.)
- My hearers should identify one morally indifferent situation about which Christians disagree and be able to think through how to act in that situation.

3. For a discussion of instructional objectives helpful to any teacher, see Robert F. Mager, *Preparing Instructional Objectives,* 2d ed. (Belmont, Calif.: Fearon, 1975).

Stage Six

Table 1

If the goal is:	Knowledge	Insight	Attitude	Skill
Then the verb can be:	List	Discriminate between	Determine to	Interpret
	State	Differentiate between	Develop	Apply
	Enumerate	Compare	Have confidence in	Internalize
	Recite	Contrast	Appreciate	Produce
	Recall	Classify	Be convinced of	Use
	Write	Select	Be sensitive to	Practice
	Identify	Choose	Commit yourself to	Study
	Memorize	Separate	Be enthusiastic about	Solve
	Know	Evaluate	Desire to	Experience
	Trace	Examine	Sympathize with	Explain
	Delineate	Comprehend	View	Communicate
	Become aware of	Reflect on	Plan	Assist in
	Become familiar with	Think through	Feel satisfied about	Pray about
	Become cognizant of	Discern		
	Define	Understand		
	Describe	Discover		
	Recognize			

- Members of the congregation should understand how God loves them and explain at least one way in which that love makes them secure.
- Christians should be able to explain what people must believe to become Christians and should plan to speak to at least one person about the Lord in the coming week.
- Listeners should be convinced of the necessity to study the Bible and should enroll in a church Bible class, a home Bible class, or a Bible correspondence course.

Framing purposes that describe measurable results forces you to reflect on how attitudes and behavior should be altered. That, in turn, will enable you to be more concrete in your application of truth to life. After all, if a sermon accomplishes anything, it must accomplish something.

David Smith, a Scottish preacher, describes a sermon as "a speech concluded with a motion." One effective means of incorporating the purpose into the sermon, therefore, lies in writing out a conclusion with the purpose in mind. State in a rough way what you are asking the congregation to do as a result of what you have preached. Be as specific as possible. If someone came to you next week and said, "I have been thinking about what you preached last Sunday, but I don't know how what you said applies to my life," would you have an answer? Picture the truth you have preached being acted upon in some specific situations. Then put that into your conclusion. Here are some examples:

- "Is there someone with whom you have a broken relationship? A spouse, a parent, a friend? As a follower of Jesus Christ, you need to take the first step today to make it right. Is there a letter you should write? Is there a phone call you should make? Is there a visit you should make or a conversation you should have? Then will you ask God for the courage to make that contact and take that step to get that matter settled?"
- "Your job is the will of God for you. Tomorrow when you go to your work, take out a Post-it note and write 'God has put

me here to serve Him today' and then place it on your desk
or in your locker—some place where you can see it easily.
Whenever you look at that note, breathe a prayer, 'Lord,
I'm working this job for you. Help me to do it to please you.'
In that way you can remember the workday to keep it
holy."

You may change the conclusion later in your preparation, but
you have determined where you purpose to go. You concentrate
your thought with greater efficiency if when you begin, you
know what you intend to accomplish.

Stage Six

New Concepts

Measurable results
Purpose
Homiletical idea

Definitions

Measurable results—the purpose of the sermon stated in terms of observable behavior.

Purpose—what one expects to happen in the hearer as a result of hearing this sermon.

Homiletical idea—the statement of a biblical concept in such a way that it accurately reflects the Bible and meaningfully relates to the congregation.

six

THE SHAPES
Sermons Take

Stages in the Development of Expository Messages

Samuel Johnson observed that people need to be reminded as much as they need to be informed. In light of his counsel, let's pause for a moment to survey the territory we have traveled. Through a study of the passage, we should have determined the exegetical idea by stating clearly what the writer was talking about and what he was saying about what he

115

was talking about. In an effort to relate the exegesis to the contemporary audience, we then probed the idea with three developmental questions:

- "What does that mean?" Explain it!
- "Is it really true?" Prove it!
- "What difference does it make?" Apply it!

From this we framed a homiletical idea that relates the biblical concept to modern men and women. In addition, we established a purpose for the sermon.

At this point, therefore, we should know what we have to preach and why we are preaching it. Now the question before us is this: What must be done with this idea to carry out the purpose? What shape will the sermon assume?

Stage 7   Thinking about the homiletical idea, ask yourself how this idea should be handled to accomplish your purpose.

Sermons develop in three major ways: deductively, semi-inductively, or inductively. In the deductive arrangement, the idea is stated completely as part of the introduction to the sermon, and then the sermon develops out of that idea. In the inductive development, the introduction leads only to the first point in the sermon, then with strong transitions each new point links to the previous point until the idea of the sermon emerges in the conclusion. Induction and deduction may be combined in a sermon. Your introduction may state only the subject of your sermon (what you are talking about), and then each point in the sermon presents a complement to the subject. Another variation of the inductive/deductive development is that in your introduction, you lead up to your first point and develop it inductively. You may do that for the second point in the sermon where you will, for the first time, give the complete statement of your idea. Once your idea has been stated, the sermon must proceed deductively to explain or prove or apply the idea. See figure 1 for a comparison of the different shapes sermons may take.

Figure 1

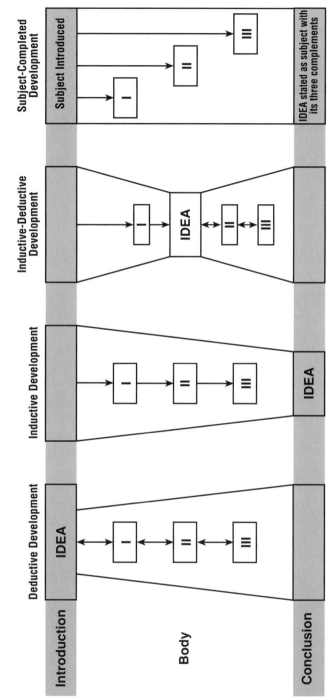

All of this may seem as clear as the instructions on the income tax form. With this overview in mind, let's look more closely at the deductive arrangements. Basically our homiletical ideas expand in line with the broad purposes of the sermon. Just as any statement we make develops through explaining, proving, or applying it, so sermon ideas, too, demand explanation, validation, or application.

Deductive sermons, therefore, can take three different forms.

DEDUCTIVE ARRANGEMENTS

An Idea to Be Explained

Sometimes an idea must be explained. That happens when you want your congregation to understand a doctrine of the Bible. A truth correctly comprehended can carry its own application. For example, if your car comes thumping to a halt because a tire has blown out, you must change the tire. If you do not know how to change it, your greatest need is for a clear explanation. Standing beside the highway, aware of the flat tire, you will actively listen to instruction on how to fix it. Having understood the explanation, you will presumably be motivated to get out the tools, jack up the car, and go about the business of trading the flat for the spare. All of this is to say that offering an audience a clear explanation of a biblical passage may be the most important contribution you can make through your sermon.

One well-worn formula for sermon development says: "Tell them what you are going to tell them; tell them what you are telling them; then tell them what you have told them." When our purpose requires that we explain a concept, that is splendid advice. In the introduction to such a sermon we state the complete idea; in the body we take the idea apart and analyze it; and in the conclusion we repeat the idea again. Certainly such a development wins through clarity anything it loses in suspense.

As an example, Alexander Maclaren preached a sermon to explain Colossians 1:15–18: "Who is the image of the invisible God, the firstborn of all creation; for in him were all things created, in the heavens and upon the earth, things visible and things invisible, whether thrones or dominions or principalities or powers; all things have been created through him, and unto him; and he is before all things, and in him all things consist. And he is the head of the body, the church: who is the beginning, the firstborn from the dead; that in all things he might have the preeminence" (ASV). Trying to make sense of this passage is difficult. You can't help but ask, "What does that mean?"

Within the sermon Maclaren states his purpose: "My business is not so much to try to prove Paul's words as to explain them, and then press them home." His subject is, "Why is Jesus Christ supreme over all creatures in everything?" and his complement is, "Because of his relation to God, to the creation, and to the church." Bringing his subject and complement together, the statement of his idea for the sermon would be, "Jesus Christ is supreme over all creatures in everything because of his relation to God, to the creation, and to the church." In developing this idea through explanation, Maclaren purposes to motivate Christians to make Christ preeminent in their lives.

How then does Maclaren go about the sermon? He offers his idea twice in the introduction. "Christ," he declares, "fills the space between God and man. There is no need for a crowd of shadowy beings to link heaven with earth. Jesus Christ lays His hand upon both. He is the head and fountain of life to His church. Therefore, He is first in all things to be listened to, loved, and worshipped by men." The entire sermon will say nothing more than that. In the next paragraph Maclaren presents the idea in an abbreviated form a second time: "There are here three grand conceptions of Christ's relations. We have Christ and God, Christ and the creation, Christ and the church, and built upon all these, the triumphant proclamation of His supremacy over all creatures in all respects."

In the body of the sermon, Maclaren explains what those relationships involve. Reduced to its outline, the sermon proceeds in this way:

> I. The relation of Christ to God is that He is "the image of the invisible God" (Col. 1:15).
>   A. God in Himself is inconceivable and unapproachable.

B. Christ is the perfect manifestation and image of God.
  1. In Him the invisible becomes visible.
  2. He alone provides certitude firm enough for us to find sustaining power against life's trials.
II. The relation of Christ to creation is that He is "the firstborn of all creation" (Col. 1:15–17).
  A. Christ is the agent of all creation, and the phrases Paul used imply priority of existence and supremacy over everything.
  B. Christ sustains a variety of relations to the universe; this is developed through the different prepositions Paul used.
III. The relation of Christ to His church is that He is "the head of the body" who is "the beginning, the firstborn from the dead" (Col. 1:18).
  A. What the Word of God before the incarnation was to the universe, so is the incarnate Christ to His church. He is the "firstborn" to both.
  B. As "the head of the body," He is the source and center of the church's life.
  C. As the "beginning" of the church through His resurrection, He is the power by which the church began and by which we will be raised.

Conclusion: "The apostle concludes that in all things Christ is first—and all things are, that he may be first. Whether in nature or in grace, the preeminence is absolute and supreme. . . . So the question of questions for us all is, 'What think ye of Christ?' . . . Is he anything to us but a name? . . . Happy are we if we give Jesus the preeminence, and if our hearts set 'Him first, Him last, Him midst and without end.'"[1]

In this entire sermon Maclaren does little else but answer the question, "What does this passage mean?" In explaining it, he applies it. In one major way Maclaren's sermon could have been stronger. In his introduction, he could have done more to show his listeners why they needed to understand this passage. Aside from not understanding it (which is a need, but not a strong one), a modern audience would wonder, "Why bring this up?"

---

1. An outline is not a sermon. To read this sermon with its supporting material, see Faris D. Whitesell, ed., *Great Expository Sermons*, pp. 68–77.

One other thing is essential in a sermon about an idea explained: your introduction is crucial to its success. You must find a need for the explanation. This sermon form works only if you scratch your people where they itch. No one listens to instructions on how to make a soufflé if he or she has never even boiled an egg.

A Proposition to Be Proved

Deductive sermons take other forms, however, and sometimes an idea requires not explanation but proof. When this is the case, the idea appears in the introduction as a proposition you will defend. Because your stance as a preacher resembles that of a debater, your points become reasons or proofs for your idea. You're answering the developmental questions, "Is that true?" and "Why should I believe it?"

An example of a sermon in which a proposition is proved can be taken from 1 Corinthians 15:12–19, where Paul argues for the resurrection of the body. In the context Paul has contended that the Corinthians cannot believe that Jesus rose from the dead and continue to maintain that there is no such thing as resurrection. A sermon from verses 12–19 will defend the proposition, "The Christian faith is worthless unless Christians rise from the dead." The preacher aims to convince the hearers that the doctrine of resurrection lies at the center of Christianity. The idea is stated in the introduction, and the major points defend it as a series of arguments. In outline form the sermon would look like this:

> I. If Christians do not rise, the Christian faith lacks valid content (vv. 12–14).
>   A. If the dead do not rise, it follows that Christ did not rise.
>   B. If Christ did not rise, then the gospel is a delusion.
>   C. If the gospel is a delusion, then our faith in that gospel has no substance.
> (A second reason why the Christian faith is worthless unless Christians rise . . .)
> II. If Christians do not rise, the apostles are despicable liars (v. 15).

A. Since the apostles all preached the resurrection of Jesus, which could not have taken place if there is no resurrection, then they are "false witnesses."

B. They are guilty of the worst kind of falsehood, since they gave false testimony about God, whom they claimed raised Jesus from the dead.

(A third argument why the Christian faith is worthless unless Christians rise . . .)

III. If Christians do not rise, then the Christian faith is futile (vv. 16–17).

A. If Christ's resurrection did not happen, which would be the case if there is no resurrection of the dead, then the effects ascribed to it are not valid.

B. Christians therefore are still dead in their sins. A dead Savior is no Savior at all.

(A fourth argument to be considered . . .)

IV. If Christians do not rise, then Christians have no hope (vv. 18–19).

A. If there is no resurrection, then Jesus was not raised and his death accomplished nothing.

B. It would follow then that dead saints "have perished."

C. Christians suffering for Christ in anticipation of life to come are to be pitied. Without resurrection, the hope that sustains them is only wishful thinking.

Conclusion: The resurrection of the dead stands as a crucial doctrine of Christianity. If it falls, the entire system of Christian faith crumbles with it, and the Christian gospel and its preachers offer nothing to the world. Since Christ has been raised, however, the belief in resurrection and the Christian faith rest on a strong foundation. We live in hope.

At first the idea explained and the idea proved appear to be identical because both sermons set forth the sermon idea in the introduction and then develop it. What must be recognized, though, is that the sermons expand in different directions to accomplish different purposes.

A Principle to Be Applied

A third form that deductive sermons take grows out of the question of application: So what? What difference does this make? In this type of sermon you establish a biblical principle in either your introduction or your first major point; then in the remainder of your message you explore the implications of the principle.

An outline of a sermon designed to apply a principle is drawn from 1 Peter 2:11–3:9. The introduction to the sermon discusses how our attitudes determine action and then asks the question, "What should be our attitude as Christ's men and women in a world that is no friend of God and grace?" The purpose behind the sermon is to have Christians develop a submissive spirit in their social relationships. The principle to be applied appears in the first point.

    I. We are to be subject for God's sake to every human institution (2:11–12, 21–25).
      A. Subjection brings glory to God (2:11–12).
      B. Christ illustrates submission even to institutions that worked evil against Him (2:21–25).
        1. He was completely innocent (v. 22).
        2. He remained silent and trusted Himself to God (v. 23).
        3. His sufferings were redemptive (vv. 24–25).

(What difference should this principle of submission to human institutions make in our daily lives?)

    II. This principle of adopting a submissive spirit for God's sake must govern us in our social relationships (2:13–20; 3:1–7).
      A. We are to submit for God's sake to civic leaders (2:13–17).
      B. We are to submit for God's sake to our employers (2:18–20).
      C. We are to submit for God's sake to our spouses (3:1–7).
        1. Wives should have a submissive spirit toward their husbands (vv. 1–6).
        2. Husbands should have a submissive spirit toward their wives (v. 7).

Conclusion: "All of you be harmonious, sympathetic, brotherly, kindhearted, and humble in spirit; not returning evil for evil, or insult for insult, but giving a blessing instead; for you were called for the very purpose that you might inherit a blessing" (3:8–9 NASB).

The three sermon forms we have discussed—an idea explained, a proposition proved, and a principle applied—are deductive arrangements of the sermon. In all three, your idea is stated in the introduction or the first major point of the sermon. Everything within the sermon, then, relates back to the idea.

There are also semi-inductive sermons. These sermons fall in between deduction and induction.

SEMI-INDUCTIVE ARRANGEMENTS

A Subject to Be Completed

The first semi-inductive form presents only the subject in the introduction, not the entire idea, and the major points complete the subject. This subject-completed form of development is the most common one used in our pulpits, and many preachers never vary from it.

In the hands of a skilled preacher, a sermon patterned this way can produce tension and strong climax. James S. Stewart, in an exposition of Hebrews 12:22–25, provides a case study. In his introduction, Stewart establishes his subject. The writer of Hebrews, he tells us, "is saying five things about our fellowship of Christian worship in the church." The purpose of the sermon is, in his words, "to make us realize the riches of our heritage when we assemble in our places of worship." With the subject "What makes our worship rich?" being stated in the introduction, each point in the body helps to complete it.

> I. It is a spiritual fellowship: "You are come unto Mt. Zion, the city of the living God, the heavenly Jerusalem" (v. 22). Christians have direct touch with that invisible spiritual world which is the only ultimate reality.
>   ("I pass on to the second fact our text underlines concerning the fellowship of Christian worship.")
> II. It is a universal fellowship: "You are come to the church of the firstborn who are written in heaven" (v. 23). Christians

are members of the greatest fellowship on earth, the Church universal.

("I pass on to the third description he gives of our fellowship in Christian worship.")

III. It is an immortal fellowship: "You are come to myriads of angels in festal array, and to the spirits of just men made perfect" (v. 23). When Christians are at worship, their loved ones on the other side of eternity are near to them and a cloud of witnesses surrounds them.

IV. It is a divine fellowship: "You are come to the God of all who is Judge, and to Jesus the mediator of the new covenant" (vv. 23–24). In your worship, he tells them—reaching now to the very heart of the matter, you have come to God as revealed in Jesus.

("One other fact about our fellowship in worship he adds, and so makes an end.")

V. It is a redeeming fellowship: "You are come to the blood of sprinkling, that speaketh of better things than that of Abel" (v. 24). "When our sins cry out to God for punishment and vengeance, something else also happens—the blood of Christ cries louder, overbears and silences the very crying of our sins, and God for Christ's sake forgives."[2]

Stewart has no formal conclusion, but rather, his final point serves to bring the sermon to an effective close. Notice that in his transitions, he relates each separate point not to the previous point but only to the subject that it completes.

This sermon form depends on a key word that holds the points together. In Stewart's sermon, it is the generic word *things*. Each of his five points is a "thing" about our fellowship when we come together to worship. One complaint about the subject-completed form of semi-inductive sermons is that it can be boring. It bores the preacher and, when it is used constantly, it can bore the audience. More important, there is a danger of imposing on the thought of the biblical writer what the writer himself is not saying. We force the thought of the passage into a previous mold.

2. The complete sermon, with its sturdy language and effective supporting material, may be found in Faris D. Whitesell, *Great Expository Sermons*, pp. 138–46.

The advantage of the form, however, is that it is simple and easy to use.[3]

Induction-Deduction

Induction and deduction may be combined in your sermon. The idea is stated some place in the middle of the sermon. The introduction and first or second point will lead up to the idea, then the remainder of the sermon proceeds deductively to explain, prove, or apply the idea.

One specific way the inductive-deductive sermon can be developed is to explore a problem. Within the introduction and first point you identify a personal or ethical problem, explore its roots, and perhaps discuss inadequate solutions. At the second point you propose a biblical principle or approach to the problem, and throughout the remainder of the sermon, you explain, defend, or apply it.

This inductive-deductive arrangement also applies to "life situation" preaching. In the introduction you discuss in personal terms a question, problem, or bewildering experience such as depression or grief. You may then demonstrate that the specific case you have brought up actually reflects a more general theological or philosophical problem. Finally, you offer a positive biblical solution in a practical, usable manner. Your sermon, therefore, becomes a bridge-building project that spans the gulf between personal needs on one side and scriptural truth on the other.

INDUCTIVE ARRANGEMENTS

Sermons can also be developed inductively. Inductive sermons move toward a complete statement of your idea at the end of the sermon. In your introduction, therefore, you do not state the complete idea of your sermon. You will relate your introduc-

---

3. For further elaboration on this form, see Charles W. Koller, *Expository Preaching without Notes* (Grand Rapids: Baker, 1962) or Faris D. Whitesell and Lloyd M. Perry, *Variety in Your Preaching*. Whitesell and Perry give several pages of different key words that can be used to achieve variety.

tion only to the first point of the sermon. Following that point, you must raise another question, directly or indirectly for the audience to consider. Your second point, then, grows out of your first point. When your second point is developed, you must raise still another question coming out of that point, which is answered in your next point. Only when all of your points have been developed will you state the idea of your sermon.

Obviously, transitions are crucial in an inductive sermon. Your audience cannot refer back to your central idea because you have not stated it. They're completely at your mercy. If your transitions do not remind them of where they have been, and the question that emerges that still must be answered, your audience is lost. If you are a fledgling preacher, proceed with caution. Congregations who have been exposed to an inductive sermon at the hands of an amateur may still be wandering around, trying to find their way home.

At the same time, inductive sermons have advantages. They produce a sense of discovery in listeners. As preachers, we often see ourselves as going to the Scriptures and finding truth and delivering it to our listeners. The sermon becomes show-and-tell. In the inductive sermon, listeners can have the experience of learning truth for themselves. It can produce a strong sense of discovery.

Inductive sermons are particularly effective with indifferent or even hostile audiences. They work well with hearers who might reject your sermon idea out of hand. Through induction you can present a series of ideas that the audience will agree with until you come to your major idea, and they are forced to accept it. This has been called the "yes-yes" approach. You will get the audience to say yes to a number of things with which they agree before you present a concept with which they will disagree. When Peter addressed the throng at Pentecost—a crowd which had recently crucified Jesus—he employed an inductive approach. In his introduction he answered the questions in the minds of his hearers about the phenomena of Pentecost. By quoting from the prophet Joel, he then went on to prove from their Scriptures and from experience that Jesus is the Christ and Lord they had murdered, the one who alone could save them from judgment. He stated his idea at the conclusion of his message: "Therefore let all the house of Israel know assuredly that God has made this Jesus, whom you crucified, both Lord and Christ" (Acts 2:36 NKJV). Had he offered that idea at the beginning of his sermon, his listeners might have killed him. Through his inductive approach, he turned a suspicious and antagonistic audience into people who asked, "What must we do?"

It is difficult to sketch the structure of an inductive sermon using a traditional outline. Because all outlines have to be deductive (a main point stated and then supported), it is easier to map an inductive sermon in a series of movements that leads up to the sermon's one major idea. Start with an honest human problem and work toward a biblical solution. Your sermon may unfold something like this:

The mess someone is in. Develop a problem in personal terms. How does a particular individual experience it? How do they actually talk about what they are going through? All theological questions show up in life somehow, somewhere, or they aren't worth the bother. Start your sermon in someone's life.

But look! This personal mess is really part of something larger. The individual's situation is really a single case of something much wider. Provide examples of where the problem shows up in different ways in people's experience. What are the consequences this larger problem creates in ourselves or in people we know? What questions does that raise?

Not only that, but the mess didn't start with us. We are talking about something fundamental to human experience. Talk about the problem as it occurred to people throughout history and particularly to someone in the Bible.

That raises a deeper question: how did anyone get into this mess? Was it deliberate? Do people stumble into it?

Folks don't go down without a struggle. What solutions have they tried to clean up the mess they were in? How did people in the Bible respond? Did the solutions work or simply make matters worse?

Finally, there must be good news. There is a way out of the mess! Expose the biblical principle at work in your passage. How did it work in men or women in the Bible? Then relate the principle to the individual you introduced in your introduction. Apply it to others wrestling with the same kind of problem.

Not all of these moves in your sermon get equal space. While it is tempting to talk about the problem, you must spend enough time showing your listeners the solution in the biblical account and the solution at work in life.

The inductive sermon is closer to a conversation than to a lecture. To make it work, we have to know how people actually think and act. Listeners have to feel "that could be me." We also have to feel our way back into the Scriptures. The difference between a religious discourse and a sermon throbbing with life is the difference between reading a book on poverty and standing in line with a mother and her three hungry kids waiting to get some food stamps. Share Paul's fury as he wrote to the Galatians. Feel a knot in your stomach over Asaph's faith-shaking doubts in Psalm 73. Smell the stench of Job's sores. Feel Timothy's anxiety in feeling overmatched and undermanned by his assignment at Ephesus. The Bible is great literature, but literature is not life. "The printed page is too free of blood and tears," Ernest Campbell noted, "to be even a reasonable facsimile of reality." Inductive sermons work best when, from beginning to end, from current problem to biblical solution, we are talking about actual people, not about cardboard characters in tissue-paper plots.

A Story Told

Inductive sermons have special appeal to inhabitants of a culture dominated by television and motion pictures. We have become a storied culture. Whether it is a mystery drama, a comedy, or even a sports contest, there is a large element of induction. The drama isn't solved until the end of the last act, and the joke leads up to the punch line, and the sports event moves toward the final score. Inductive sermons fit that way of thinking. That is particularly true of a specific type of inductive sermon—a story told. You connect with a modern audience when you tell a biblical story with insight and imagination.

Unfortunately, through some tortured reasoning we have per-

Stage Seven

suaded ourselves that stories belong to children and that mature adults take their principles straight, without any sugar coating. Therefore we relegate stories to the nursery or we carry a novel with us on vacation only as a way to pass the time.

The low marks we have given to the story must be revised upward if we observe the impact stories make upon us all. Television abounds with them—some shoddy, some shady, some shaky, some worthwhile—but TV dramas attract audiences and shape their values. The future of our culture may depend on the stories that capture the imagination and mind of this generation and its children.

Anyone who loves the Bible must value the story, for whatever else the Bible is, it is a book of stories. Old Testament theology comes packaged in narratives of men and women who go running off to set up their handmade gods, and of others who take God seriously enough to bet their lives on Him. When Jesus appeared, He came telling stories, and most of them have entered the world's folklore. In fact, so brilliant a storyteller was Jesus that we sometimes miss the profound theology disguised in His tales of a rebellious delinquent and his insufferable brother, a pious Pharisee and a repentant tax collector, buried treasures, and a merchant who had an unexpected appointment with death.

Narrative preaching however does not merely repeat a story as one would recount a pointless, worn-out joke. Through the story you communicate ideas. In a narrative sermon, as in any other sermon, a major idea continues to be supported by other ideas, but the content supporting the points is drawn directly from the incidents in the story. In other words, the details of the story are woven together to make a point, and all the points develop the central idea of the sermon.

Narratives are most effective when the audience hears the story and arrives at the speaker's ideas without the ideas being stated directly.

Motion picture director Stanley Kubrick discussed the power of the indirect idea in an interview reported in *Time*: "The essence of dramatic form is to let an idea come over people without its being plainly stated. When you say something directly, it is simply not as potent as it is when you allow people to discover it for

Stage Seven

themselves."[4] Whether the points are stated or only implied depends on your skill as the preacher, the purpose of your sermon, and the awareness of your audience. In any case the story should unfold so that listeners identify with the thoughts, motives, reactions, and rationalizations of the biblical characters, and in the process acquire insight into themselves as well.

We have looked at several forms sermons can take. Some are deductive, others are inductive, and still others fall some place in between. What we have surveyed should not be considered exhaustive but suggestive. In the final analysis, there is no such thing as "a sermon form." God's truth would be better served if we didn't think about preaching a sermon at all. When we have arrived at what we believe is the meaning of a passage and have thought about the needs and questions of our audience, then the question is, What is the best way for this idea to be developed? The shoe must not tell the foot how to grow; therefore, ideas and purposes should be allowed to take their own shape in your mind. To test a form, you should ask at least two questions: (1) Does this development communicate what the passage teaches? (2) Will it accomplish my purpose with this audience? If your development communicates your message, by all means use it; if it gets in the way of your message, then devise a form more in keeping with the idea and purpose of the Scriptures and the needs of your hearers.

When an architect designs a building, he or she begins with a concept derived from function (what the building is to do) and form (how the building will look). To construct the building, the architect turns the idea into a blueprint showing in detail how the concept will translate into steel, stone, and glass.

Stage 8 Having decided how the idea must be developed to accomplish your purpose, outline the sermon.

When you have derived a concept from the biblical data and shaped it toward your audience's need, you must now fashion a

---

4. In Martha Duffy and Richard Schickel, "Kubrick's Grandest Gamble," *Time*, 15 December 1975, p. 72.

blueprint, which is the outline of your sermon. Although content may exist without form, structure provides a sermon with a sense of unity, order, and progress. Certainly no sermon ever failed because it possessed a strong outline.

The outline is for your benefit. Congregations do not hear outlines. They hear a preacher speaking. Your outline, therefore, serves you in at least four ways. First, you view your sermon as a whole, and therefore, you heighten your sense of unity. Second, the outline clarifies in your eye and mind the relationships between the parts of your sermon. Third, your outline also crystallizes the order of ideas so that you will give them to your listeners in the appropriate sequence. Finally, you will recognize the places in your sermon that require additional supporting material that must be used to develop your points.

Sometimes the arrangement of ideas in the biblical passage will have to be altered in the outline. The biblical writer did not have your audience in mind. He may have followed an inductive order; but because of your hearers, you may select a deductive plan. Sermons based on the epistles fit more easily into outlines than do poems, parables, or narratives. Unless you remain flexible in the ways you communicate passages, you will find it impossible to accomplish the purpose of some passages with your audience. If you were to handle the epilogue of Proverbs, for example, you will discover that the passage cannot be outlined logically. Proverbs 31:10–31 consists of a Hebrew acrostic describing the qualities of a wise woman from *aleph* to *tav*, the A to Z of the Hebrew alphabet. This is a summary of the virtues of wisdom detailed in Proverbs now fleshed out in life experience. Although the acrostic is an effective memory device for a Hebrew reader, it becomes sheer nonsense for English listeners. To teach this passage, therefore, you must place your own outline upon its subject matter.

Outlines usually consist of an introduction, a body, and a conclusion.

- The introduction (which will be discussed in greater detail) introduces the idea, the subject, or in the case of inductive sermons, the first point.
- The body of the outline then elaborates on the idea.
- The conclusion (also to be treated later) brings the idea to a focus and ends the sermon.

The sermon is made up of a multitude of ideas, all related to one another. Not all ideas in a sermon have equal importance. Some are more basic than others. The most fundamental ideas become the main points and make up the basic framework around which the sermon is built. These main points stand as Roman numerals in the body of the message. For example:

IDEA: Christians should praise God because of all that He has done for us.
   I. We should praise God because He has elected us in Christ (Eph. 1:4–6).
   II. We should praise God because He has dealt with us according to the riches of His grace (vv. 7–12).
   III. We should praise God because He has sealed us with the Holy Spirit until we acquire full possession of our inheritance (vv. 13–14).

Simply listing these major points, however, does not completely develop the sermon. Because main points need expansion, secondary points elaborating the main points are added to the outline. We use capital letters to designate these supporting points and, in addition, we indent them.

   I. We should praise God because He has elected us in Christ (Eph. 1:4–6).
      A. He elected us before the foundation of the world (v. 4).
      B. He elected us because He preappointed us to sonship through adoption (v. 5).
      C. He elected us so that He would be praised for the glory of His grace (v. 6).

The addition of these subpoints improves the outline by making the development clearer and more specific. The outline can be even more complete if it brings in specific details to support your secondary points. We usually use an Arabic number and further indentation to show subordination of these details to the secondary points. In the sample outline the sermon expands by the addition of detail.

> II. We should praise God because He has dealt with us according to the riches of His grace (Eph. 1:7–12).
>   A. He has remitted our sins through Christ's blood (v. 7).
>   B. He has given us wisdom to understand the mystery of His will (vv. 8–10).
>   1. His will is according to His good pleasure which He purposed to carry out in Christ (vv. 8–9).
>   2. His will purposes to unite all things in Christ at the proper time (v. 10).

With each expansion of the outline, the substance of the sermon becomes more obvious. An individual who had never looked at the passage in Ephesians could read the outline and gain some idea of the speaker's organization and development of the sermon.

If you need additional development, you show it by the use of small letters and further indentation. A sermon outline, in contrast to one for a thesis or research paper, should be simple and have relatively few points. A complicated outline broken into several indented subdivisions, while impressing the eye, will only bewilder the preacher as it is preached and the audience as it listens.

Keep in mind that each point in the outline represents an idea and thus should be a grammatically complete sentence. When only words or phrases stand as points, they deceive us because they are incomplete and vague. Partial statements allow thought to slip through our minds like a greased football. While you may carry an abbreviated outline into the pulpit, you will find that it fails you if you use it in your study.

There is something else to remember: each point should be a declarative sentence, not a question. Questions do not show relationships because they are not ideas. The points in your outline should answer questions, not raise them. Questions may be used in the delivery of your sermon as transitions introducing new points. You may include these transitional questions before your point, and in your outline they are placed in parentheses.

While you see your outline lying before you on the page, remember that your congregation does not hear an outline. It hears only the content of the outline. This obvious fact makes transitional statements particularly significant because they point up relationships of the parts to the whole. You must help your listeners separate your major points from the material that supports them. That's why it takes at least three or four statements and restatements of a point to make a point clear to an audience. Carefully constructed transitions help your listeners to think with you so that together you and they move through the sermon. An effective transition notifies the audience that you are moving on. You will often review where you have been, identify the thought to which you are moving, relate what has been said to the main subject or idea, and interest the hearer in the thought that is to follow.

Because clear transitions don't spring readily into the mind, they should be planned in advance. Effective transitions state or imply the logical or psychological connection between the introduction and the body, the points within the body, and the body and the conclusion. They answer the question, Why these points in this order? Some transitions linking the subpoints of your sermon may accomplish this with just a few words, but other major transitions may require a paragraph to establish the unity, order of points, and movement in the sermon. While transitions should be written out and included in parentheses in the outline, you will often amplify and enlarge on them even more as you actually preach the sermon.

Stage Eight

New Concepts

Deductive arrangement
Inductive arrangement
Semi-inductive arrangement
Some forms sermons take:
    Idea explained
    Proposition proved
    Principle applied
    Story told
    Subject completed
Outline
Transition

Definitions

Deductive arrangement—the idea appears as part of the introduction, and the body explains, proves, or applies it.

Idea explained—the idea is presented in the introduction, and the points of the sermon are steps in the explanation of the idea.

Inductive arrangement—the introduction introduces only the first point in the sermon, then with a strong transition each new point links to the previous point until the idea emerges in the conclusion.

Outline—shows the speaker the relationship between the ideas of the sermon. You can tell at a glance which ideas are superior, subordinate, and coordinate.

Principle applied—the idea is stated in the introduction or first point as a principle of faith or life. The remainder of the sermon applies that principle to daily experience.

Proposition proved—the idea is stated in the introduction like the proposition of a debate. The points are proofs of that proposition.

Story told—a story of Scripture is narrated in such a way that the idea is developed directly or by implication.

Subject completed—the subject of the sermon appears in the introduction. The main points of the sermon are complements of that subject.

Transition—notifies the audience that the preacher is moving on by stating (or occasionally by implying) the logical or psychological connection between the introduction and the body, the points within the body, and the body and the conclusion.

For Further Reading

If you want to explore inductive sermons further, you might start with *Inductive Preaching: Helping People Listen* by Ralph and Greg Lewis (Wheaton: Crossway, 1983). Fred Craddock also presented the case for inductive preaching in his thought shaping book *As One without Authority* (Nashville: Abingdon, 1979). For some specific instruction in how to prepare a narrative sermon, including the first-person narrative sermon, read *Variety in Biblical Preaching* by Harold Freeman (Waco: Word, 1987). Paul Borden answers the question, "Is There Really One Idea in That Story?" and shows you how he crafts it in chapter 5 of *The Big Idea of Biblical Preaching*, edited by Keith Willhite and Scott Gibson (Grand Rapids: Baker, 1998). Daniel Buttry offers ten of his first-person sermons, along with comments on how he prepared and preached them, in *First-Person Preaching* (Valley Forge, Pa.: Judson, 1998). You will also find an assortment of narrative sermons in my book *Biblical Sermons* (Grand Rapids: Baker, 1989). Eugene Lowry, in *Doing Time in the Pulpit* (Nashville: Abingdon, 1985), argues that any sermon can be plotted with strong narrative qualities.

Verse-by-verse preaching, another sermon form, has fallen out of fashion in recent years. Perhaps it has failed as much in the hands of its friends as at the hands of an enemy. Verse-by-verse preaching resembles playing a saxophone—it is easy to do poorly. A defense of running commentary preaching, however, comes from two authors who are card-carrying "new homileticians." It is *Preaching Verse by Verse* by Ronald J. Allen and Gilbert L. Bartholomew (Louisville: Westminster/John Knox, 1999). This little book not only defends verse-by-verse preaching, but also demonstrates how to do it.

seven

MAKING

Dry Bones Live

Stages in the Development of Expository Messages

Outlines serve as skeletons of thought, and in most sermons, as in most bodies, the skeleton will not be completely hidden. We ought not put the outline on vulgar display, however, as if the skeleton were "Exhibit C, Victim of Starvation." The most effective means of hiding the bare bones of a sermon is not by disposing of the skeleton but by covering it with flesh.

Supporting material is to the outline what skin is to bones or walls are to the frame of a house.

Stage 9   Fill in the outline with supporting materials that explain, prove, apply, or amplify the points.

An audience does not respond to abstract ideas, nor have many people ever been moved to faith by reading an outline of Romans. If an outline remains undeveloped, therefore, an audience can miss its meaning and remain unconvinced. As the sermon unfolds, listeners raise several questions: "I wonder what he means by that?" "What evidence does she have for that statement?" "Sounds interesting, but how would this work out in my life?" "I didn't catch that. Would you say that again?" To amplify, explain, prove, or apply your ideas and make them understandable and appealing, you use a variety of supporting materials.

RESTATEMENT

We have already talked about restatement during our discussion of transitions. Restatement, saying the same thing in different words, is used in other places in your sermon. Restatement serves at least two purposes. First, it helps you make a concept clear. Listeners, unlike readers, must get what you say when you say it. A reader who is confused by what she is reading can flip back a few pages and pick up the author's flow of thought. But listeners have no such option. If at first they don't understand you, then unless you say it again in other words, the listener is lost.

Restatement differs from repetition. Repetition says the same thing in the same words; restatement says the same thing in different words. Repetition may profitably be used throughout the sermon like a refrain to reinforce a major idea, but the skillful preacher learns to restate a point several times in different ways. Restatement resembles the blinking cursor on the computer. It shows listeners where they are. Restatement is like marching in place. It does not have forward movement, but it is part of the parade. It is saying the same thing in different words.

Clovis G. Chappell employs restatement in his introduction to a sermon on the woman taken in adultery (John 8:1–11). "The scholars are uncertain as to where in the sacred record this story belongs. Some think that it does not belong at all. From certain of the ancient manuscripts it is omitted. However, speaking not as a scholar but merely as a Bible reader, I am sure that it does really belong. Here I feel is a true story. If it is not true, it is one from which the truth itself might learn. Not only is this story true, but in my judgment it is factual. It is the record of an event that actually took place. It would have taken a superb genius indeed to have invented a story so true to life. Certainly it is consistent with what we know about the scribes and the Pharisees; it is yet more consistent with what we know about Jesus himself."[1]

All that Clovis Chappell is saying in this paragraph of thought is, "I think this story really happened."

Peter Marshall emphasizes a point through restatement in his sermon "The Art of Moving Mountains":

I am sure that each of you has read this statement many times:
Prayer Changes Things
You have seen it painted on posters which adorn the walls of our Sunday school rooms.
You have seen it stamped on little metal plates,
read it in the Bible,
heard it from the pulpit, oh, so many times.
But do you believe it?
Do you actually, honestly, believe that prayer changes things?
Have you ever had prayer change anything for you?
Your attitudes
your circumstances
your obstacles
your fears?[2]

Restatement, then, makes your concepts clear. Listeners may not get the meaning of your point when you say it for the first

---

1. Clovis G. Chappell, *Questions Jesus Asked* (New York: Abingdon-Cokesbury, 1948; reprint, Grand Rapids: Baker, 1974), p. 154.
2. Peter Marshall, *John Doe, Disciple: Sermons for the Young in Spirit*, ed. Catherine Marshall (New York: McGraw-Hill, 1963), p. 144.

time, but when you restate it in different words, that can cause them to say, "Oh, I see what you mean."

Restatement serves a second purpose: it also impresses an idea on the listener's mind. If you say something once, it can be ignored, but if you repeat it several times, it will influence a hearer's thoughts and feelings. Advertisers invest millions of dollars to restate their ideas on radio, on television, and in magazines. You need to develop that skill as well.

DEFINITION AND EXPLANATION

A definition establishes limits. It sets down what must be included and excluded by a term or statement. When we think of definitions, we usually think of dictionaries where we find terse, quick explanations of a word.

Explanation, like definition, also sets boundaries, but it may do so by amplifying on how ideas relate to one another or what an idea implies. Notice how Earl F. Palmer explains what is meant by the Greek word *eros*:

> *Eros* is love that is earned, love that is won from us. It is not the instinctive love that we have for our parents or our children, our family or our social or racial structure. It is not the kind of love we have for something like wisdom or mankind. It is love earned from us because of the compelling excellence of the person or thing or reality. It is the love of beauty, the love of power, the love of strength.[3]

Definitions and explanations work in a variety of ways. We usually define a term or idea by placing it in a broad class of things of which it is a part. At the same time, however, we must show how it differs from other things in that class. Classification, therefore, explains both similarities and differences. Palmer says, "*Eros* is love [the broad class of which it is a part] that is earned, love that is won from us [how it differs from other kinds of love]."

3. Earl F. Palmer, *Love Has Its Reasons: An Inquiry into New Testament Love* (Waco: Word, 1977), pp. 38–39.

Sometimes we define and explain through synonyms. A synonym works, however, only if it touches listeners' previous experience and makes them understand and feel the meaning intended. Presumably everyone knows what cults are; but perhaps they don't know in the particular way we want, so we may say, "The cults are the unpaid bills of the church."[4]

Comparison and contrast also help us develop and explain ideas. Palmer used both in his explanation of *eros*.

Illustrations, too, help us to explain. Ray C. Stedman did this when he asked in a sermon, "What do we mean when we say a thing is holy? Look at your Bible and it says, 'Holy Bible.' What makes it holy? The land of Israel is called, 'The Holy Land' and the city of Jerusalem is called, 'The Holy City.' Why?" Then he answers, "There is a quality about all three which they share in common. They all belong to God. The Bible is God's book; Israel is God's land; Jerusalem is God's city—they are God's property! That is why they are holy; they belong to God."

Explanation proves to be more difficult if you do not know your audience. The more familiar you are with a subject, the less aware you may be of a congregation's ignorance of it. Most people in the pews live in a different intellectual world from yours. Indeed they support you financially so that you can study what they cannot. You must not assume that your listeners immediately understand what you are talking about. You owe them a clear explanation of exactly what you mean. It is obvious that we should not use jargon or language that is unnecessarily abstract. If you must use theological language, you should define every important term in language the audience understands. Certainly it is better to define too many terms than too few. In explaining the relationships and implications of ideas, you should know the explanation yourself so clearly that no vagueness exists in your mind. Then you should work through the steps in the explanation so that they come in a logical or psychological order. A mist in the pulpit can easily become a fog in the pew.

---

4. This often-quoted statement appears, for example, in Anthony A. Hoekema, *The Four Major Cults* (Grand Rapids: Eerdmans, 1963), p. 1.

FACTUAL INFORMATION

Facts consist of observations, examples, statistics, and other data that may be verified apart from the speaker. You make a factual statement when you declare, "Greek is a rich and varied language having several words for love. But only two of these words, *philia* and *eros*, exerted much influence in Greek literature or thought in the first century." If your listeners cared to do so, they could verify the accuracy of that statement by checking the words the Greeks used for love. In the expository sermon, observations about the content of a passage are factual because hearers can see for themselves what the Bible says.

Much that parades as fact is opinion in disguise. "As a matter of fact," a preacher says, "the greatest threat to the morality of America is the television set." Of course that is not a matter of fact at all, only a matter of opinion. That opinion may or may not be valid, depending on the facts. Facts, of course, are stupid things until they are brought into relationship with each other and conclusions are drawn from them. Opinions, on the other hand, are just as stupid unless they are built on facts. The expositor, like any ethical speaker, needs to know the facts and be sure of their validity. "Every man has a right to his own opinion," Bernard Baruch observes, "but no man has a right to be wrong in his facts." Facts not only help the listener understand, but when used correctly, they secure respect for the speaker.

Statistics are a special form of facts that enable us to survey a large amount of territory very quickly. They are particularly appealing to citizens in a numbers-conscious society. Indeed, the American appetite for statistics seems insatiable, and statisticians crank out an unending supply, ranging from the number of hours an average family watches TV to the percentage of unhappy marriages in our culture. This allegiance to numbers has created its own pitfalls for the innocent—and opportunities for the dishonest. An air of certainty hangs over the decimal point or the fractionalized percentage, even where measurement is unknowable or absurd. A classic illustration is a report made years ago that one third of all women students at Johns Hopkins University had married faculty members. The percentage was accurate. Johns Hopkins had only three women students at the time, and one of them married a faculty member. The statistics were accurate, but the statement is misleading. Preachers eager to win their point may be particularly susceptible to the unsupported statistic. One evangelist reported, "I read not long ago that 50 percent of heavy-metal groups practice devil worship and witchcraft, and I believe the figure is rising each day." Who counted? Who was counted? When? Where?

When statistics do enter a sermon, they should be as simple as possible without sacrificing accuracy. Round numbers are usually sufficient. While an accountant might be impressed with the information that in 1950 the population of Chicago was 3,620,962, most of us will find the figure "a little over three and a half million" easier to grasp. As we work with statistics, data can be made meaningful and vivid by comparing them to things within the experience of the audience. In describing the temple of Diana in Ephesus, we might say, "It was 180 feet wide, over 375 feet long, with columns that towered 60 feet in height," and then add, "That temple was wider and longer than a football field including the end zones, and the columns were taller than a five-story building." A speaker made understandable the small size of an electron by first giving the decimal fraction, which was incomprehensible, and then adding: "If an electron were increased in size till it became as large as an apple, and a human being grew larger in the same proportion, that person could hold the entire solar system in the palm of his hand and would have to use a magnifying glass in order to see it." Wow!

QUOTATIONS

We introduce quotations to support or expand a point for two reasons: impressiveness and authority. When we discover that someone else has stated the idea more effectively than we can, we use the other person's words. James S. Stewart introduces a sermon on Isaiah 5:30 with a snatch of a phrase from Robert Browning: "Of all the doubts which, as Browning puts it, can 'rap and knock and enter in our soul,' by far the most devastating is doubt of the ultimate purpose of God." Stewart develops his introduction with a series of other quotes, all selected because of the power of their wording. He says:

> . . . that is precisely the doubt which is lying like an appalling weight on multitudes of lives to-day. They would think twice before subscribing to Tennyson's faith:
>
> *Yet I doubt not thro' the ages one increasing purpose runs,*
> *And the thoughts of men are widen'd with the process of the suns.*
>
> "Where is any evidence of such a purpose?" they want to ask.
> . . . So they are back where Ecclesiastes was. "Vanity of vanities, all is vanity." What is the use, cried Thomas Hardy, of all your prayers, you praying people, when you have nothing better to pray to than
>
> *The dreaming, dark, dumb Thing*
> *That turns the handle of this idle Show?*
>
> "A bad joke"—that was Voltaire's final verdict on life. "Ring down the curtain," said the dying actor, "the farce is done."[5]

There are many ways to talk about the place pain plays in our lives. A preacher sums up one perspective by quoting words more impressive than his own: "Pain plants the flag of reality in the fortress of a rebel heart."

Anchoring a point with some wording that digs into the mind is probably the major reason preachers turn to quotations in sermons. When we give credit for that kind of quote, we do so primarily for ethical reasons.

We also include quotations to gain authority. In this case, when we give credit for what we quote, we do so because the person who said it is in a better position to speak than we are. Ernest T. Campbell does this in speaking of times when the seeming futility of what we do causes us to draw back from involvement in social action. Campbell reported:

---

5. James S. Stewart, *The Gates of New Life* (New York: Scribner, 1940; reprint, Grand Rapids: Baker, 1972), pp. 1–2.

I was struck the other day by Leonard Woolf's view of his life's work. "I see clearly," he said, "that I have achieved practically nothing. The world today and the history of the human anthill during the past 5–7 years would be exactly the same as it is if I had played ping pong instead of sitting on committees and writing books and memoranda. I have therefore to make a rather ignominious confession that I must have in a long life ground through between 150,000 and 200,000 hours of perfectly useless work."[6]

We also quote others because they are in a better position to know the facts or interpret them or because the audience would be more likely to accept their evaluation. Who says something makes a difference. Quoting a fundamentalist preacher on the importance of proclaiming God's judgment resembles quoting a Muslim on the virtues of the Koran. He is expected to take up that cause. It is much more arresting to quote John Steinbeck on the subject. In his *Travels with Charley,* he described a Sunday visit to a New England church. The minister delivered a no-nonsense fire-and-brimstone sermon. The noted author reflected favorably on the experience:

For some years now, God has been a pal to us, practicing togetherness, and that causes the same emptiness a father does playing softball with his son. But this Vermont God cared enough about me to go to a lot of trouble kicking the Hell out of me. He put my sins in a new perspective. Whereas they had been small and mean and nasty and best forgotten, this minister gave them some size and bloom and dignity. I hadn't been thinking very well of myself for some years, but if my sins had this dimension, there was some pride left. I wasn't a naughty child but a first-rate sinner, and I was going to catch it.[7]

At other times, an expert is better qualified to speak with authority on a subject. D. M. Baillie calls in a historian, T. R. Glover, to demonstrate that early Christians possessed an intellectual quality in their faith:

6. Ernest T. Campbell, *Locked in a Room with Open Doors* (Waco: Word, 1974), p. 117.
7. John Steinbeck, *Travels with Charley: In Search of America* (New York: Bantam, 1966), p. 78.

Dr. T. R. Glover, who was such an authority on that period [the early centuries A.D.], tells us that one reason why Christianity conquered the world was because it did better thinking than the rest of the world. It not only knew better how to live and how to die: it also knew better how to think. It "out-thought" the world. Here is a deeply interesting passage: "The Christian read the best books, assimilated them, and lived the freest intellectual life the world had. Jesus had set him free to be true to fact. There is no place for an ignorant Christian. From the very start every Christian had to know and to understand, and he had to read the Gospels, he had to be able to give a reason for his faith. They read about Jesus, and they knew him, and they knew where they stood. . . . Who did the thinking in that ancient world? Again and again it was the Christian. He outthought the world."[8]

Authorities must carry credentials. Several questions should be asked about experts to establish competence:

1. Does experience or training qualify them to speak with authority on this subject?
2. Is the testimony based on firsthand knowledge?
3. Is the authority prejudiced? Prejudiced authorities do not inspire trust because they will tend to look with favor on evidence supporting their opinions and to overlook the rest. Prejudiced authorities speaking *against* their bias can, of course, make an excellent witness. An agnostic or atheist speaking on behalf of Christianity would be strong support because he is expected to speak against it.
4. How does the audience regard the testimony? Do they know the witness? Do they respect her? When an obscure individual is used as an authority, we should tell the audience what qualifies that person to speak to the issue.[9]

Quotes should be used sparingly. Sermons ought not sound like term papers. As a general rule, quotes should be brief.

8. D. M. Baillie, *To Whom Shall We Go?* (New York: Scribner, 1955; reprint, Grand Rapids: Baker, 1974), pp. 62–63.
9. Alan H. Monroe, *Principles and Types of Speech*, p. 233.

Long quotations often become unclear and hinder communication. Sometimes a longer quote may be paraphrased and then a few important sentences from the quotation read directly to the audience.

Introduce your quotations into the sermon with a touch of freshness. It requires little effort to draw in a quote with "Spurgeon said," "Paul wrote," or "the Bible says." More thought is demanded but more accomplished if we set them up: "Written boldly into the Bible is this phrase . . ." "Paul felt keenly that . . ." "This is what Charles Dickens was trying to tell us when he observed . . ." "You can see the significance of those words embedded in verse 10 . . ."

NARRATION

When we gossip, we don't gossip about ideas, but about people. When popular newsmagazines such as *Time* handle complex subjects, such as the economy or political upheaval in China, they do so in part by featuring the people involved. Narration within a sermon describes the individuals and events embedded in biblical accounts. Every passage has its people—sometimes they stand out in the open laughing, cursing, plotting or praying, and at other times they play hide-and-seek and we must look for them. In every text, though, there is always somebody writing and somebody reading. Pull aside a doctrine and you'll find personalities. For example, grace does not exist in cold storage in heaven. There is only someone giving grace and another receiving it.

The men and women in Galatia never thought of themselves as "legalists." They felt they were devoted to the Old Testament and probably could not figure out why Paul was so upset with them. The Holy Spirit knew the value of narration when He filled the Scriptures with it, and Jesus demonstrated the impact of narration in the parables He told.

You can use narration in a sermon to supply background by filling in the history, setting, or the actions and spotlighting the personalities involved. John Hercus allowed us to live with David as he wrote Psalm 24:

> David sat up straight, stretched his arms and yawned. It had been a day of rehearsing, going over the whole processional routine with the musicians, the singers, and the ballet. The score and the choreography were well advanced, and David was more than satisfied. The psalm was good—short, clear, well-suited to the occasion. Hm-m-m-m-m . . . that was a choice phrase about "ascend the hill of the Lord . . . stand in His holy place." Very good. It would make a fine background for work with the cymbals and trumpets and chorus. And the ballet would have splendid chances, under his leadership, to express their rising feeling of spiritual drama.
>
> And those four conditions of entry into the holy place—they were just right. Terse, compact, neat. Clean hands, pure heart, no accent on trashy values (that's really what he meant by "does not lift up his soul to what is false") and no cheating or being deceitful. Yes, indeed, that checks a man out as fully and completely as you could wish.
>
> Clean hands . . . like his own clean hands . . .
>
> Suddenly a memory flashed into his mind. A memory of washing, washing, washing those "clean" hands of his, trying to scrub away a bloody thing that could not be undone. How did it happen? Oh yes . . . because of Michal.[10]

Narration takes on energy when your verbs and nouns paint pictures on your listeners' minds. A different viewpoint often brings freshness to an oft-told account. How did the woman taken in adultery or the woman at the well think of Jesus when they first met Him? In the epistles, Paul pictures an objector jumping up to argue with him: "What advantage . . . is there in being a Jew?" (Rom. 3:1 NIV), someone asks. "Food for the stomach and the stomach for food" (1 Cor. 6:13 NIV), argues a hedonist of the time. What were they like? Can you describe how they might have carried on the discussion?

Use dialogue. The Gospel narratives and the parables are filled with it. Put words into people's mouths. When only one person

10. John Hercus, *David*, 2d ed. (Chicago: InterVarsity, 1968), pp. 55–56.

appears, use soliloquy or "self-talk." That's what Hercus did with David, and it's what Jesus did with the shrewd branch manager (Luke 16:2–7) and the destitute boy in the far country (Luke 15:11–32). The lad asks himself, "How many hired servants of my father's have bread enough and to spare, and I perish here with hunger!" (v. 17 ASV).

Narration means communicating with imagination, and imagination reflects the insights of faith. Imagination is half brother to interpretation because both relate to the text. In interpretation, we determine what the passage means from what the passage says. In the same way, imagination goes one step beyond the biblical facts and yet stays tied to them.

ILLUSTRATIONS

S. I. Hayakawa's advice for speakers wanting to develop clarity is to study a cookbook, because recipes explain general concepts by breaking them down to their specifics. A recipe for beef Wellington reads: "Place tenderloin on rack in open roasting pan. Do not add water. Do not cover. Roast in a 425 degree oven, 20 to 25 minutes." Hayakawa's counsel is particularly helpful for specialists, whose extensive knowledge of a subject can keep them from being effective communicators. Their education moves them away from particulars to the vague realms of abstraction.

Theologians, for example, may speak about *hamartiology* instead of *sin* because the abstract word serves as a better umbrella for the varied aspects of the topic. When theologians address an audience less familiar with their discipline, though, they must step down from their abstraction and talk about murder, lying, stealing, or adultery. If they cannot or will not do this, though they may get high marks as scholars, they fail as communicators. Søren Kierkegaard complained that when he asked the philosopher Georg Hegel for directions to a street address in Copenhagen, all he received was the map of Europe.

Skilled preachers deal in high and low levels of abstraction, climbing back and forth like laborers on a ladder. To have meaning, particulars must be gathered up in generalizations, and abstractions must be taken down to particulars to be made understandable. "The interesting writer, the informative speaker, the accurate thinker, and the sane individual, operate on all levels of the abstraction ladder, moving quickly and gracefully in orderly fashion from higher to lower, from lower to higher—with minds as lithe and deft and beautiful as monkeys in a tree."[11]

One means of bringing your sermons down to life lies in the use of illustrations. Well-chosen, skillfully used illustrations can do just about everything—restate, explain, validate, or apply ideas by relating them to tangible experiences. To fix a truth firmly onto the hearer's mind requires that we state it and state it again. While most restatement comes through the repetition of propositional statements, illustrations can present the truth still another time without wearying the listeners. Understanding, too, may be gained through analogies and anecdotes. An illustration, like the picture on television, makes clear what the speaker explains.

Illustrations also make truth believable. Logically, of course, examples cannot stand as proof, but psychologically they work with argument to gain acceptance. If you wanted to argue that all truth is equally valid but not equally valuable, you might use an analogy to get your audience to accept what you are saying. A penny and a dollar bill are both genuine, you may point out, but they are not of equal worth. Therefore we must distinguish between penny- and dollar-truth. The analogy wins as much agreement as the reasoned argument.

Illustrations also apply your ideas to people's experience. Your listeners need not only to understand a biblical concept, but they also need to know what difference it makes. Examples display truth in action. William E. Sangster preached a sermon based on Genesis 41:51 that developed the idea, "We must remember to forget." He concluded his sermon with an anecdote:

> It was Christmas time in my home. One of my guests had come a couple of days early and saw me sending off the last of my Christ-

11. S. I. Hayakawa, *Language and Thought in Action*, p. 190.

mas cards. He was startled to see a certain name and address. "Surely, you are not sending a greeting card to him," he said.

"Why not?" I asked.

"But you remember," he began, "eighteen months ago . . ."

I remembered, then, the thing the man had publicly said about me, but I remembered also resolving at the time with God's help, that I had remembered to forget. And God had "made" me forget!

I posted the card.

People today need applications that show them "how to do it," and they need plenty of them. The seasoned faithful need help. What about those souls who may be the product of dysfunctional families or who have bypassed the church on their way to growing up and come into faith out of cold secularism? They often lack the skills needed for living a life of faith. They need us to draw them a picture. If a father is not "to provoke his children to anger," how exactly does he do that or keep from doing it? It's a dandy idea to trust God in a crisis, but what might that look like in practice? We are urged to "confess our sins," but how do you go about it, and are you talking about every one of them? The Scriptures teach us that if a brother or sister "repents," we are to forgive them. In a Bill Watterson comic strip, the cartoon character Calvin says to his tiger sidekick, Hobbes, "I feel bad that I called Suzie names and hurt her feelings. I'm sorry I did it." "Maybe you should apologize to her," Hobbes suggests. Calvin ponders this advice and then replies, "I keep hoping there's a less obvious solution." Calvin needs Hobbes to help him do what was right. So do those who come to listen to us.

Lynn Anderson, in his helpful book *If I Really Believe, Why Do I Have These Doubts?*, uses an illustration to apply the concept that the living Word of God is self-validating:

> Jesus said, "It is more blessed to give than receive." "Well," you say, "that is a nice theory—but is it really true?" There is really only one way to find out: *Give!* Give generously and consistently, and before long you will begin to experience the blessings of being a great giver. And when that happens, you can say, "Hey, I *know* that that is true!"

Sharon found out firsthand that the lifestyle of faith fits. A few years ago Sharon's faith was on hold. She felt she should contribute more to God's work, but she didn't really feel like it. Besides she really didn't think she had anything important to give—or that anyone would want her "gift." Sharon did want more faith, however. So she committed to teach a fourth-grade Sunday school class.

But there's a little more to this story. Sharon has multiple sclerosis and lives in a wheelchair. Just getting around is a chore in itself. She knew the hassle of transporting her teaching materials to and from her house, car, and classroom could overwhelm her, but Sharon wanted to do what faith would do.

That was several years ago! Today Sharon is a valued member of a strong teaching team. Her kids adore her—and they have learned a lot about handicaps too. . . . Sharon has found that doing what faith would do "fits." New feelings of self-worth and trust in God's care have blessed her with a vastly improved quality of life.[12]

It takes effort to think of ways a great truth may be applied to life. Sometimes you have an illustration from your life and ministry. At other times you can imagine a situation that someone in your audience might go through where a biblical insight might be used. Be as specific as possible. Fill in the details so that people respond, "Oh, I *see* what you mean!" Sermons cannot always be a "how to" manual, of course, but sermons seldom fail because they are specific. Too many of us preach sermons that are all cork and no pop.

Illustrations serve you and your congregation in other ways. They aid memory, stir emotion, create need, hold attention, and establish rapport between speaker and hearer.[13]

The foundational principle for the use of illustrations is that illustrations should illustrate.

To illustrate is a transitive verb. It takes an object. An illustration should illustrate something. Therefore, there is no such

---

12. Lynn Anderson, *If I Really Believe, Why Do I Have These Doubts?* (West Monroe, La.: Howard, 2000), p. 166.

13. Ian MacPherson lists seventeen purposes served by illustrations in *The Art of Illustrating Sermons*, pp. 13–33.

thing as "a good illustration," but only a good illustration of a particular truth. According to its etymology, to illustrate means "to throw light on a subject." Illustrations resemble a row of footlights that illuminate the actors and actresses on the stage. If a footlight shines into the eyes of the audience, it blinds them to what they ought to see.[14] A story told for its own sake may entertain or amuse an audience, but it gets in the way of your sermon. An anecdote works in the service of truth only when it centers attention on the idea and not on itself.

Illustrations should also be understandable. Through examples, we clarify the unknown with the known. If you need to explain an illustration to make it clear, you should not use it. To explain an illustration which, in turn, explains a concept is to use the unfamiliar to illustrate the unfamiliar. Examples taken from the Bible sometimes violate this rule because we illustrate the unknown with the unknown. In a day of biblical illiterates, biblical stories may be as remote to modern listeners as ancient Chinese history. If we use them as illustrations of other biblical passages, we may indulge in an exercise of futility. If you tell stories from the Bible, then you must take time and care to relate them so that an audience can enter into them and feel their force. You are usually better off illustrating a biblical truth from modern life. Because you want to illuminate the unknown by the use of the known, your most effective illustrations will touch as close to the lives of your listeners as possible. Human interest stories have great power because they deal with subjects out of our common experiences, such as children, animals, and comic strip characters.

Some illustrations are more effective than others. Effective communication is more like a handshake than an E-mail message. It is something we experience as well as hear. The best illustrations not only appeal to people's minds, but also touch their emotions. The strongest examples flow out of our lives into the listeners' lives.

Think of two large overlapping circles. The circles represent your life and the life of your listener (see figure 2). Within each large circle there is another circle. This smaller circle represents

14. John Nicholls Booth, *The Quest for Preaching Power*, p. 146.

everything you have personally experienced—the dog you grew up with, the friends you had, the games you played, the high school you attended, your first date. The outer circle, on the other hand, represents the things you have read about, seen in a movie, watched on television, heard about in school. Some of these, such as a vivid movie, feel very close to the inner circle. Other things, such as an event in the eighteenth century, lie much further away. Your listener, too, has an inner circle and an outer circle, representing actual experiences and vicarious experiences.

Figure 2

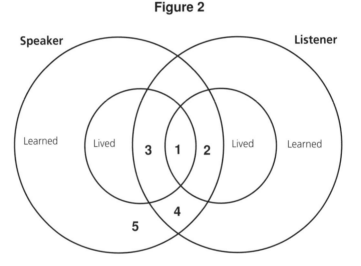

1) The speaker's and listener's lived experience overlap.
2) The speaker's learned experience overlaps the listener's lived experience.
3) The speaker's lived experience overlaps the listener's learned experience.
4) The speaker's learned experience overlaps the listener's learned experience.
5) The speaker's lived or learned experience does not overlap the listener's lived or learned experience.

The most powerful illustrations are those where your personal experience overlaps your listener's personal experience. Examples drawn from these circles we call human interest stories. These illustrations make us laugh, weep, or wince because we have been there, done that, and have the T-shirt to prove it.

The second-best illustrations are those where your learned experience overlaps your listener's lived experience. When possible, we want to talk into our audience's lived experiences. Pastors of rural churches who grew up in the city must learn as much as possible about farmers and farming if they expect to illustrate their sermons effectively for their congregations.

The third-best illustrations come out of the speaker's direct experience and overlap the listener's vicarious experience. A minister who grew up on a farm and is speaking to an urban congregation can tell a story about delivering a calf so vividly that even a city audience can identify with it.

The fourth and least effective illustrations speak from the speaker's learned experience into the audience's learned experience. Illustrations from the Puritans, the life of Woodrow Wilson, or Alexander the Great fall into this category. The audience may understand the illustration, but listeners will not experience it.

The fifth level of illustration is stories that do nothing in the hearer. They fall completely outside the listener's awareness. The preacher illustrates an abstract truth with some incident completely unknown to the audience. It may be possible with time and effort to bring the incident into the congregation's outer circle. But why bother? The aim of an illustration is to explain the unknown with the known, the distant with the familiar. These stories do not communicate. The basic principle of illustration has been completely ignored. Usually biblical incidents used to illustrate other passages fall into this category. Modern congregations do not know their Bibles, and even when they do, the stories sound like part of the long-ago-and-far-away, distant from life as they live it.

Jay Adams adds an additional warning about biblical illustrations: they are often not biblical. "Always use the Bible authoritatively; never illustratively. Scripture was not given to illustrate points; it was written to make points. If you don't pay attention to this warning, the first thing you know, you will find yourself making points you want to make and using (misusing) the Bible to illustrate and back up your ideas."[15]

Illustrations should also be convincing. As much as lies in you, be sure of your facts. Although a factually inaccurate story might illustrate your idea, if you use it with an audience aware of the error, you will undermine your credibility. What is more, illustrations ought not offend the good sense of an audience. Truth may be stranger than fiction, but improbable anecdotes leave your audience to suspect that you are strange. If you must use an incident that seems far-fetched, acknowledge that and then give your authority for it. Let someone else shoulder the blame.

Ministers seem to beget children who talk in illustrations. When you tell too many such stories about your bright and witty children, skeptical congregations cannot help but wonder whether you're always telling them the truth. Something else: because personal illustrations can have great force, you can succumb to the temptation of relating stories as though they happened to you, when in reality they did not. The gospel sits in judgment on the methods used to proclaim it, and ultimately God's truth cannot be benefited by our falsehoods. If a congregation suspects that we will lie to make a point, they have good reason to believe that we will also lie to make a convert.

Your illustrations should be appropriate to the theme of your sermon and to your audience. Great truth can be trivialized by your illustrations. A student preacher, eager to emphasize the omnipresence of God, declared, "God is even in that trash can." What his illustration had in accuracy, it lacked in appropriateness. Some illustrations, acceptable to one audience, might not be appropriate for another. For example, this story, while reflecting on the morality of our age, would have to be weighed for its appropriateness for different groups:

A man sat in a restaurant, chatting with an attractive young woman. In the course of the conversation, he pointed to a well-dressed young man seated at a corner table.

15. Jay Adams, *Preaching with Purpose* (Grand Rapids: Zondervan, 1981), p. 10.

"See that fellow over there? If he offered you $500 to go to bed with him tonight, would you do it?"

"$500?" the young woman responded. "Well, for $500 I guess I would."

A few minutes later, the man pointed to another fellow seated in another part of the room.

"See that guy over there? Suppose he offered you $20 to spend the night with him. Would you do it?"

"$20?" she sniffed. "Of course not! What do you think I am?"

The man replied, "I've already found that out. I'm just trying to establish your price."

That illustration might be acceptable on a college campus or in a talk to businesspeople, but you would have to consider carefully whether or not it would be appropriate for a Sunday morning congregation.

Tell your illustration with energy and enthusiasm. A sculptor was once asked how he carved a statue of a lion when he didn't have a model. He explained, "I simply carved away anything that didn't look like a lion." That is good advice for preachers, too. A skillful storyteller cuts away surplus details that don't contribute to the mood or punch line of the story. When you use an illustration that contains narrative, use dialogue and direct quotation. Don't simply retell the story. Relive it. Get into it. If you see the action in the story, so will your audience. Tell your stories as vividly as possible so that your listeners enter into the illustration, understand it, and feel it. When that happens, not only is your point being made—it is being felt.

Where do you find them? Good illustrations can be found everywhere. Start with your personal experience. Every life is a circus. Some people can find more illustrations in a stroll around the neighborhood than others can find in a trip around the world. The difference lies not in what we experience but in what we see in our experience. You must observe in order to see. The world can be God's picture book if in ordinary events you see analogies, applications, or spiritual truth.

Personal illustrations add warmth and vitality to a sermon, but to use them effectively, keep three general rules in mind.

- First, as we've already said, the illustration should be true. Don't say something happened to you if it didn't.
- Second, the illustration should be modest. Congregations dislike first-person stories when the preacher emerges regularly as the hero. We react negatively to conversational bores who brag about how clever, humorous, or spiritual they are. That reaction doesn't change when boasting is done from the pulpit. Most of our experiences, of course, make us neither victors nor villains, and they can be recounted with modesty and great benefit. If you use a personal illustration, do so without apology. If a preacher says, "If you will pardon the personal illustration . . ." attention is directed to what should not be noticed at all. If the incident should be used, then there is no need for an apology. If it should not be used, then an apology will not help.
- The third rule that must be scrupulously observed when using personal illustrations is that you must not violate a confidence. People will resist sharing a concern with their pastor if they wonder whether they will appear as part of next week's sermon. Even when a personal incident can be shared without hurting or embarrassing anyone, ask permission to use it. Even though you may feel you're flattering people, they may resent the public exposure.

Not only can illustrations be gathered from your personal experience, but they also can come out of your reading. Few of us have memories lined with Velcro. We can't afford to read without a pen in hand to record materials that can some day illuminate our sermons. All kinds of reading qualify—comic strips, nursery rhymes, magazines, novels, theologies, history—all provide material for sermons. Read sermons by gifted preachers. Such sermons provide illustrations in context, and that makes them superior to collections of stories which are divorced from what they illustrate.

Of course, many illustrations will occur to you as you work on your sermon. Write down clearly the point you want to make, and then think of the parts of that point that require illumination. You must know exactly what you want to illustrate if you expect your mind and memory to supply what you need. Your ability to fashion appropriate analogies and apt applications will be sharpened through practice.

Undoubtedly, the place to which you will turn most often for supporting material is your illustration file. Of course, what you get out of your file for a given sermon depends entirely on what you have put into it. There are many systems on the market developed to enable ministers to save the results of their study and reading. You will probably want to keep two kinds of illustration files:

- One is a letter-sized file in which you store sermon notes, booklets, or even pages torn from unwanted books. This file may be broken down according to subjects and the different books of the Bible. You might check with a local seminary library for the system it uses to catalog its collection and adapt their system to your use.

- In addition to a large letter-sized file, you might also consider a smaller 3" x 5" card file. One section of this file may be divided into the books of the Bible, with the cards arranged under each book according to chapter and verse. In this section of the file you can store illustrations, exegetical notes, or bibliography pertaining to particular passages of Scripture. Sometimes you will find in a commentary on Romans a helpful insight into a passage in Genesis. Add this to your Scripture file. Another section of your 3" x 5" card file can be indexed according to subjects. One way to break down the subject file is by using the first letter and the first vowel of the subject:

Aa	Ae	Ai	Ao	Au
Ba	Be	Bi	Bo	Bu
Ca	Ce	Ci	Co	Cu

Illustrations on the subject of "atonement" would be filed under AO—the first letter and the first vowel in the word.

The advantage of this system lies in its simplicity and versatility. Most material that you will want to keep as supporting material in a sermon—anecdotes, quotes, poems, exegetical notes, analogies, bibliographic references—can be filed on 3" x 5" cards.

This is the twenty-first century. Another way to file supporting material is on your computer. There are several different software programs that can be adapted for a preacher's use. Now that computers have become smaller and therefore portable, you can carry your system with you.

You need a filing system. Any system that allows you to store information is superior to no system at all. Your filing system also needs you. No system works unless you determine to work it. Agur, a writer of proverbs, commends the ant for its great wisdom: "The ants are not a strong people, yet they prepare their food in the summer" (Prov. 30:25 NASB). You will do well to learn that lesson from the ant.

New Concepts

Repetition
Restatement
Explanation
Definition
Factual information
Quotations
Narration
Illustrations

Definitions

Definition—establishes what must be included and excluded by a term or statement.

Explanation—sets boundaries by amplifying the relation of one idea to another or what an idea implies.

Factual information—consists of observations, examples, statistics, and other data that may be verified apart from the preacher.

Narration—describes who did what to whom with what effect in the biblical accounts. It can be used to supply background in a sermon by discussing the history, setting, or personalities involved in a passage.

Illustrations—restate, explain, prove, or apply ideas by relating them to tangible experiences.

For Further Reading

There are scores of books on illustrations. Most books on homiletics treat these collections as though they were pornography. If you order one by mail, they imply, you should have it wrapped in plain brown paper. They rightly argue that the danger in these volumes lies in using them as "Saturday night specials." Stories grabbed in desperation usually sound canned and contrived.

I believe, however, that books of illustrations do have a place in your library. To avoid abuse, here's a suggestion: read through those books at your leisure and mark those that strike you as effective. Put them in your personal file. If you use them at a later time, they have a better chance of being as fresh as material you have gathered on your own. Here are a few collections you might want to look at.

- R. Kent Hughes went through his file and put together *1001 Great Stories and Quotes* (Wheaton: Tyndale, 1998). Not all of them are "great," but many are worth using.
- *Illustrations for Biblical Preaching*, edited by Michael Green (Grand Rapids: Baker, 1989), is a particularly helpful collection of analogies and stories waiting to be turned into illustrations.
- Ed Rowell, in *Fresh Illustrations for Preaching and Teaching* (Grand Rapids: Baker, 1997), has gathered over 200 illustrations from *Leadership Journal* that are a couple of notches above average.

Of course, the best illustrations are still those that you gather from your own living and reading.

eight

START WITH A BANG
and Quit All Over

Introductions and conclusions have significance in a sermon out of proportion to their length. During the introduction an audience gains impressions of you, the speaker, that often determine whether or not they will accept what you say. If you appear nervous, hostile, or unprepared, they are inclined to reject you. If you seem alert and friendly, they decide you are an able person with a positive attitude toward yourself and your listeners. Your introduction, therefore, introduces your congregation to you. In the final analysis, listeners do not hear a sermon. They hear you. While it has always been important for hearers to like a speaker, it is particularly true today. Men and women in our culture value relationships, and they will make a judgment about you and your attitudes before they will give their attention to what you have to say.

Stage 10 Prepare the introduction and conclusion of the sermon.

THE INTRODUCTION

Not only does an introduction introduce you to the audience, but your introduction should introduce your audience to the subject of your sermon idea, to your central idea, or in the case of an inductive sermon, to your first major point. The characteristics of effective introductions grow out of that purpose.

An Effective Introduction Commands Attention

An introduction should command attention. When you step behind the pulpit, you dare not assume that your congregation sits expectantly on the edge of the pews waiting for your sermon. In reality they are probably a bit bored and harbor a suspicion that you will make matters worse. A Russian proverb offers a bit of wise counsel to the preacher: "It is the same with men as with donkeys: whoever would hold them fast must get a very good grip on their ears!" The opening words of a sermon therefore need not be dramatic; they need not even be plain; but they must go after the minds of the hearers to force them to listen. If you do not capture attention in the first thirty seconds, you may never gain it at all. Producers of television dramas know this well. The action starts immediately. Only later on do we get titles or names of actors and actresses. Producers are aware that the audience sits in front of a screen with clickers in their hands. If they do not catch attention, then viewers are off to seventy-five other channels to find something else. When people come to church, they come with clickers in their heads. If you do not get their attention fast, they may be off to the menu for dinner, to a baseball game in the afternoon, or to some conflict they're having at work.

Writers have been struggling since Homer to define the art of opening a story. Charles Dickens in *The Tale of Two Cities* had a memorable opening: "It was the best of times, it was the worst of times." Some publishers believe that readers buy books on the strength of the opening paragraph. Herman Melville in *Moby Dick* opens with three words: "Call me Ishmael." Leo Tolstoy in *Anna Karenina* grabs our minds with: "Happy families are all alike; every unhappy family is unhappy in its own way." Amy Tan has an arresting opening in *The Kitchen God's Wife*: "Whenever my mother talks to me, she begins the conversation as if we were already in the middle of an argument." You cannot help but wonder what will follow when Joseph Heller starts *Catch–22* by saying, "It was love at first sight. The first time Youssarian saw the chaplain, he fell madly in love with him." So a sermon resembles a conversation between you and your audience. Based on your opening, your listeners decide if they are interested in pursuing the conversation any further.

The possibilities for an opening statement that gets attention are as wide as your creativity.

- You may start with a paradox: "Many children of God live as though they were orphans."
- You may use a familiar thought in an unfamiliar setting: "'Honesty is the best policy.' When a person says that, he may not be honest at all. He may simply be shrewd."
- Rhetorical questions reach for attention: "If it were possible for God to die and He died this morning, how long would it take you to find out?"
- A startling fact or statistic may charm your audience into listening: "One out of three marriages ends in the divorce court. Only one marriage in six is happy."
- Having read your text, you can make a provocative comment about it: "There is a delicious touch of humor about

this text. Jesus is deadly serious, but that fact does not inter-
fere with his laughter."[1]

- At times a touch of humor can win attention: "A business-
  man, completing his annual checkup, was assured by his
  physician, 'Sir, you're as sound as a dollar!' The man
  fainted."

- Your passage itself can be the basis of attention: "For many
  people Hebrews chapter six is the most perplexing passage
  in the Bible." Occasionally you may go directly to the passage: "This morning I'd like to begin by making a confession.
  I'd like to bring you the message of another preacher. That
  is, after all, the way Solomon, the author of Ecclesiastes, introduces himself."

- All of us sit up and listen at the prospect of a story: "Mary
  Watson was a housewife in her late thirties. She thought of
  herself as young and still attractive even though she had
  been married fifteen years and was the mother of three children. In the space of a month she developed into an ugly,
  old woman."

- At other times you will drive directly to your subject with a
  confrontive statement: "If you claim to be a Christian, you
  must believe in the Trinity."

However you begin, make the most of your first twenty-five or
thirty words to seize attention. An ear-grabbing opening is a clue
that what follows may be worth thirty minutes of everyone's time.

An Effective Introduction Uncovers Needs

An effective introduction should also uncover needs. You
must turn voluntary attention into involuntary attention.
When you start, the people listen because they ought to listen,
but before long, you must motivate them to listen because they
can't help but listen. Paul O'Neil, a writer for *Life* magazine,
evolved O'Neil's Law: "Always grab the reader by the throat in

---

1. Clovis G. Chappell, *Questions Jesus Asked* (Nashville: Abingdon, 1948; reprint,
Grand Rapids: Baker, 1974), p. 30.

the first paragraph, sink your thumbs into his windpipe in the second, and hold him against the wall until the tag line."[2] Social scientist Arthur R. Cohen concluded that when audiences receive information that meets felt needs, two things happen: (1) more learning takes place; and (2) opinions change faster and more permanently than when information is given and then applied to life.[3] All of this says that the important point of contact with a congregation lies in answering, "Why bring this up? Why do I need to listen?"

Charles R. Swindoll began a sermon on 2 Corinthians 1:3–11 by raising a question that exposes the raw nerve of need:

El Tablazo looked so close. Too close. It happened so fast. Exploding into the jagged 14,000-foot peak, the DC–4 disintegrated with a metallic scream.

What was left of the Avianca Airline flight bound for Quito, Ecuador, flamed crazily down the mountainside into a deep ravine. One awful moment illuminated a cold Colombian mountain in the night, then the darkness returned. And the silence.

Before leaving the airport earlier that day, a young New Yorker named Glenn Chambers hurriedly scribbled a note on a piece of paper he found on the floor of the terminal. The scrap was part of a printed advertisement with a single word, "Why?" sprawled across the center.

Needing stationery in a hurry, Chambers scrawled a note to his mother around the word in the middle. Quickly folding this last-minute thought, he stuffed it in an envelope and dropped it in a box. There would be more to come, of course. More about the budding of a lifelong dream to begin a ministry with the *Voice of the Andes* in Ecuador.

But there was no more to come. Between the mailing and the delivery of Chambers' note, El Tablazo snagged his flight and his dreams from the night sky. The envelope arrived later than the news of his death. When his mother received it, the question burned up at her from the page—Why?

2. In George P. Hunt, "Editor's Note: Attila the Hun in a Tattered Sweater," *Life*, 13 November 1964, p. 3.

3. Arthur R. Cohen, "Need For Cognition and Order of Communication as Determinants of Opinion Change," in *The Order of Presentation in Persuasion*, by Carl I. Hovland, et al. (New Haven: Yale University Press, 1957), pp. 79–97.

It is the question that hits first and lingers longest. Why? Why me? Why not? Why this?[4]

Need can be touched quickly. Asking "Can a woman who works be a good mother? What do you say? What does the Bible say?" touches need in less than twenty words.

Sermons catch fire when flint strikes steel. When the flint of a person's problem strikes the steel of the Word of God, a spark ignites that burns in the mind. Directing our preaching at people's needs is not merely a persuasive technique; it is the task of the ministry. Leslie J. Tizard understood what preaching must be about when he declared, "Whoever will become a preacher must feel the needs of men until it becomes an oppression to his soul."[5]

Needs take many shapes and forms. Christians differ from non-Christians not in their needs but in the ways their needs are met. Abraham H. Maslow, a noted psychologist, believes that needs build on one another. Throughout our lives we move from one cluster of needs to another as motivations for our actions.[6] One basic set of needs, he argues, springs from our bodies. These physiological needs are met by food, drink, recreation, sexual expression, and elimination, and if they are not met, they dominate thought and life.

Men and women also have needs that result from living with other people. These social-dependency needs include the desire for esteem, love and affection, security, self-realization, and self-expression. People want to know that they are loved, that they have worth, that they can grow, develop, and realize their potential.

On another level, people also need to have their curiosity satisfied. Maslow maintains that curiosity as a strong motivation comes only after physical and social-dependency needs have been met. In your introduction you may touch the need in your audience to have their curiosity satisfied. But you should be

4. Charles R. Swindoll, *For Those Who Hurt* (Portland: Multnomah, 1977).

5. Leslie J. Tizard, *Preaching: The Art of Communication* (London: Allen and Unwin, 1958), p. 22.

6. Abraham H. Maslow, *Motivation and Personality*, 2d ed. (New York: Harper and Row, 1970).

aware that satisfying curiosity does not cause people to respond at the same depth as when they understand how God meets their longing for self-esteem, security, affection, and love. The more basic the need, the stronger the interest.

Early in the sermon, therefore, your listeners should realize that you are talking to them about themselves. You raise a question, probe a problem, identify a need, open up a vital issue to which the passage speaks. Contrary to the traditional approach to homiletics, which holds the application until the conclusion, application starts in the introduction. Should preachers of even limited ability bring to the surface people's questions, problems, hurts, and desires to deal with them from the Scriptures, they will bring the grace of God to bear on the agonizing worries and tensions of daily life.

An Effective Introduction Introduces the Body of the Sermon

Introductions should orient the congregation to the body of the sermon and its development. *To introduce* is a transitive verb. An introduction must introduce something. Therefore there is no such thing as "a good introduction," there is only a good introduction of a particular sermon. To put it another way, an introduction should introduce. At the very least it should introduce the sermon's subject so that no one needs to guess what the preacher plans to talk about. If the subject alone is introduced, then the major points usually complete it. For example, if you raise the question, "How can we know the will of God?" the audience expects that the major assertions of the sermon will provide steps to the answer.

The introduction may go beyond the subject and orient hearers to the main idea. An exposition of Romans 1:1–17 that raises the issue of what must be done to evangelize society may lead to the statement, "When the effect of the gospel is all-important in the church, then the force of the gospel is unstoppable in the world." Once you state your complete idea, however, you must then raise one of these basic questions about it: What does this mean? Is it true? What difference does it make? While you may not use these exact words, you must raise one of these questions to expand your idea. If you fail to do so, directly or indirectly, the sermon is over even though you speak for another thirty minutes. Effective sermons maintain a sense of tension—the feeling that something more must be said if the message is to be complete. When the tension goes, the sermon ends. Therefore, through the developmental questions you explore what must be done with your idea in the remainder of your sermon. You may develop it as an idea that needs to be explained, a proposition that must be proved, or a principle that has to be applied to life.

If your sermon is to be developed inductively, then your introduction introduces your first main point. As far as your audience knows, the first point is the idea of the entire message. As the message develops, your first point must then be linked to your second point by a strong transition. This transition serves like another introduction. It raises a question or uncovers a need that comes out of your first point. It leads the listeners into the second point. In the same way, your second point must be linked to the third. In an inductive sermon, your complete idea emerges only in the final movement of the sermon.

An Effective Introduction May Exhibit Other Characteristics

An effective introduction must get attention, uncover needs, and orient the listeners to the body of the message. These characteristics are non-negotiable. There are other factors that usually appear in good introductions. For example, most introductions are contemporary. They start in the twenty-first century A.D. and not in the twenty-first century B.C. Ultimately, we are using the Bible to talk to people about themselves. We're not talking to them about the Bible. Since the object of the sermon is the listener, the beginning of the sermon grapples with the needs of the contemporary audience. It is a matter of accurate reporting, however, to say that this is not always true. Some sermons talk immediately about the biblical text. They raise questions, give arresting descriptions, or point to needs in the biblical settings that clearly reflect similar needs today. But you must have good reason to start your sermon in the ancient world rather than in the modern world.

The strongest introductions will usually be personal. While you may quote statistics about broken homes and broken marriages in our society, you will have a stronger introduction if you also talk to the people in front of you about their marriages. A sermon on relationships in the family will have greater force if you're talking about the arguments that people in front of you have had with a spouse three weeks ago that have not been resolved. Men and women will listen if they feel you are talking about the strains and temptations they feel as they try to keep their marriage vows. At times, however, you will back off from being personal because it is so forceful. If in the introduction people feel afraid or upset or angry with what you're saying, they may close their ears to anything else in the sermon. So as a general rule that has exceptions, the strongest introductions are personal.

Other things may be said about introductions. Don't open your sermon with an apology. When we use an apology, we hope to win sympathy. But at best, we gain pity. A congregation is seldom persuaded by someone for whom they feel sorry. If you are less prepared than you want to be, let the congregation discover it for themselves. In many cases they will never find out.

Keep the introduction short. After you get water, stop pumping. Unfortunately, no percentages will help you here. Most introductions take about 10 percent of the sermon time, but your introduction needs to be long enough to capture attention, uncover needs, and orient the audience to the subject, the idea, or the first point. Until that is done, the introduction is incomplete; after that is done, if you continue, the introduction is too long. An old woman said of the Welsh preacher John Owen that he was so long spreading the table, she lost her appetite for the meal.

An introduction should not promise more than it delivers. When it does, it is like firing off a cannon to shoot out a pea. Sensational introductions to mediocre sermons resemble broken promises. When you fail to meet the need you have raised, the congregation feels cheated.

Someplace at the opening of the sermon, you will usually read your text. Some ministers place the Scripture reading immediately before the sermon because the sermon should be an exposition of the passage. Unfortunately, unless the text is read skillfully, congregations may regard it as a necessary exercise that comes before they settle down to hear what is said about the Bible. As a general rule, if your text is short, read it following your introduction. When you do this, you give the audience a mindset that helps them pay attention to the reading. If you read your text before you introduce your sermon, you will help your congregation if you give them "glasses" for the reading.

For example, if you were to introduce a reading from James 2:1–13, you might introduce it by saying, "We don't often preach about ushers, but they play a crucial part in any church. In James 2, James describes a church service that went wrong because the usher didn't do things right. Listen to what James says." People will read the text in a more discerning way. There is a subtle benefit in doing this. When people know what they are looking for as you read the text, they often discover that they can read the Bible for themselves. Understanding the Scriptures is not something reserved for the professional elite.

What about humor? The simple answer is "handle it with care." If it directs the listener's attention to the idea, then laughter serves as a useful tool. If it merely entertains, humor can make the sermon feel like a letdown. Sometimes when you're speaking to a new audience, humor helps you to build a bridge, but too many jokes may cause listeners to write you off as a comedian. When humor is used, therefore, it should be used deliberately. It should relate the audience to you or to your message.

How you step into the pulpit tells your audience a lot about you. If you move in an unhurried, confident manner, your body language communicates that you are in control of yourself and that you have something important to say and that the audience would do well to listen. Before you speak, you should pause several seconds to capture attention. You and the congregation ought to start together even though you might not finish together. Look at the people, not at your notes or even at your Bible. In private conversation, if someone does not look you in the eye, you feel uneasy. That is also true when you speak to people from the pulpit.

When you are nervous, tension can make your voice high and squeaky. Therefore you need control in order to speak your opening words in a composed, relaxed manner. Take a deep breath before you start. As you begin, use a large, definite gesture after the first couple of sentences. Large gestures will direct nervous energy into positive bodily movement. You will find that nervousness and tension will also be reduced if you know before you get on your feet exactly how you will begin the sermon.

Before you speak, there are things you can do to relax your throat. For example, while you're in your study, move your head slowly to touch your left shoulder, then move it slowly in the other direction to touch your right shoulder. Do that four or five times. Then slowly turn your head as far as you can to the left, then turn your head as far as you can to the right. Repeat that several times. Finally, let your head fall on your chest and then slowly roll it to the back and then to your chest again. Repeat that exercise five times. While you're waiting to get into the pulpit, run your tongue to the back of your mouth. Try to lick your tonsils. Or yawn with your mouth shut. All of these exercises will help you to relax your throat.

There are three types of preachers: those to whom you cannot listen; those to whom you can listen; and those to whom you must listen. During the introduction the congregation usually decides the kind of speaker addressing them that morning.

THE CONCLUSION

An experienced pilot knows that landing an airplane demands special concentration, so an able preacher understands that conclusions require thoughtful preparation. Like a skilled pilot, you should know where your sermon will land.

In fact the conclusion possesses such importance that many ministers sketch it after they have determined the sermon idea and the purpose for preaching it. Whether or not you use that technique, you must work on your conclusion with special care. Otherwise everything comes to nothing.

The purpose of your conclusion is to conclude—not merely to stop. Your conclusion should be more than a swipe at getting out of an awkward situation: "May God help us live in the light of these great truths." It should be more than asking the congregation to bow in prayer so you can sneak off the platform when they're not looking. You should conclude, and the conclusion should produce a feeling of finality. Like an able lawyer, a minister asks for a verdict. Your congregation should see your idea entire and complete, and they should know and feel what God's truth demands of them. Directly or indirectly, the conclusion answers the question, "So what? What difference does this make?" And your people face another question as a result of an effective conclusion: "Am I willing to allow God to make that difference in my experience?" Big band leader Paul Whiteman understood the demands of introductions and conclusions when he advised, "When you begin, start with a bang, and when you quit, quit all over!"

Depending on the sermon, the audience, and the minister, conclusions take different shapes and forms. Because the element of freshness adds interest to preaching, work to vary your conclusions. What are some elements used to land a sermon and to bring it to a burning focus?

A Summary

In many conclusions preachers look back over the terrain and restate the major points covered along the way. When you do this, however, review the important assertions so that you can bind them into the major idea of the sermon. A good summary ties loose ends together. It should not be a second preaching of the sermon.

An Illustration

An anecdote that summarizes the idea or better shows how it works out in life adds impact to a conclusion. The illustration must hit the bull's-eye so that the listeners grasp its meaning in a flash without explanation. When you have offered the illustration, stop. The illustration should be so transparent that only a sentence or two need to be added. It has even more power when the illustration needs no explanation at all.

Peter Marshall ends a sermon on James 4:14 with a gripping story:

> An old legend tells of a merchant in Bagdad who one day sent his servant to the market. Before very long the servant came back, white and trembling, and in great agitation said to his master: "Down in the market place I was jostled by a woman in the crowd, and when I turned around I saw it was Death that jostled me. She looked at me and made a threatening gesture. Master, please lend me your horse, for I must hasten away to avoid her. I will ride to Samarra and there I will hide, and Death will not find me."
>
> The merchant lent him his horse and the servant galloped away in great haste. Later the merchant went down to the market place and saw Death standing in the crowd. He went over to her and asked, "Why did you frighten my servant this morning? Why did you make a threatening gesture?"
>
> "That was not a threatening gesture," Death said. "It was only a start of surprise. I was astonished to see him in Bagdad, for I have an appointment with him tonight in Samarra."
>
> Each of us has an appointment in Samarra. But that is cause for rejoicing—not for fear, provided we have put our trust in Him who alone holds the keys of life and death.[7]

A Quotation

Sometimes a well-chosen quote used in your conclusion can state the sermon idea in words stronger and more vivid than you can craft yourself. If you use a quotation, it should be short, and you should have it memorized. Long quotations are difficult to read well, and at a moment when you need directness, a long quote becomes indirect. A few lines taken from a poem or hymn may capture the truth of your sermon effectively. Generally, poetry, too, should be brief, as well as clear and to the point. When

---

7. Peter Marshall, *John Doe, Disciple: Sermons for the Young in Spirit,* ed. Catherine Marshall (New York: McGraw-Hill, 1963), pp. 219–20.

a hymn is quoted and then sung by the congregation, its impact may be doubled. Sometimes a single verse of Scripture, taken from the text you have expounded, may sum up your entire sermon and even apply it. When that verse is quoted at the end of an exposition, its force, strengthened by the sermon, can nail the truth to a listener's mind.

A Question

An appropriate question, or even a series of questions, can conclude a sermon effectively. A sermon on the Good Samaritan ended: "Let me conclude where I began. Do you love God? That's splendid. I'm glad to hear that. A second question: Do you love your neighbor? How can we talk about loving God whom we have not seen if we do not love our brothers and sisters and our neighbors whom we do see? If you do love your neighbors, do you mind if I ask them?"

A Prayer

A prayer can make a fitting conclusion, provided it is an honest petition and not a device to summarize the sermon or make an indirect application to the audience. When a desire for God's work emerges from a response to the sermon, then it can be expressed in an earnest prayer. For example, at the end of a sermon on the publican and Pharisee, the preacher, without calling the people to prayer, cried, "O God, be merciful to us, the sinners. Amen."

Specific Directions

On my desk in my office I have a bit of doggerel. It reports that:

> As Tommy Snooks and Bessie Brooks
> Were walking out on Sunday,
> Said Tommy Snooks to Bessie Brooks,
> Tomorrow will be Monday.

While this may rank as the ultimate low in social conversation, for a preacher it ranks high.

What can your people do to carry out the truth of Sunday morning's sermon in Monday morning's world? Your conclusion can answer that: if you do not face this question for your congregation, they may not be able to answer at all. Although some people stumble over biblical truth because they ask the question *why*, far more fail to apply biblical truth to their lives because they cannot answer the question *how*. Ask yourself this question: If people in my congregation took this idea seriously, how would it work in next week's world? Could they use it where they work? Does it make any difference in the kitchen? Or the bedroom? Does your idea have much application for a teenager struggling with peer pressure? Does it have anything to say to a couple facing retirement? Does your idea speak any word to people overwhelmed by grief who would rather not be in the service at all, but have come only out of a sense of the routine? In other words, take a trip through your congregation, and ask yourself, "How would people apply this biblical truth to the way they live?" Then, for God's sake and for their sake, tell them!

Not every sermon can end with "how to do it." Some preaching explores great questions and it accomplishes its purpose when people gain understanding of how God works in the world. No clear specific duty can be spelled out. At times the only proper response to a great biblical text is to fall down and worship. Yet your preaching will more likely be incorporated into the structures of people's lives when you offer practical suggestions on how to translate scriptural truth into life experience.

Visualization

In the mountain passes of the Pacific Northwest, highway signs warn motorists, "Beware of Falling Rock." The signs seem to be an exercise in stupidity. If those massive boulders tumble from their resting places, it is usually too late to dodge them.

Not all truth can be acted on immediately. Much of our preaching prepares people for "falling rocks" that may crash in upon them in some indefinite future. Visualization is a method that projects a congregation into the future and pictures a situation in which they might apply the truth that we have preached.

Visualization takes on force if the situation it envisions is possible, or better still, probable. Listeners can imagine themselves in that situation or one like it before it takes place. In concluding a sermon on work that has as its basic idea, "Remember the workday to keep it holy," you might visualize a scene like this:

> If you take this truth seriously, you may face difficult days ahead. Sometime in the future, you will have a boss tell you to do something that you know is wrong. He or she may urge you to falsify your spending account: "It's all right to be honest," your boss tells you, "but your overactive conscience is making other people in the department look bad." You know, however, that you ultimately will not give an account to others in the department; you will recognize that you'll give an account to God. In as polite and gracious way that you know how, you will say, "I'm sorry. I simply cannot do that."
>
> You may discover that your boss does not appreciate your commitment to honesty. In a short time, through trumped-up charges, you may lose your job. If that happens, you will feel overwhelmed. You will not be tempted to sing a cheery chorus. You'll be threatened. You'll wonder about your future.
>
> Perhaps in those grim hours, you'll remember the truth of this text. Your master is in heaven. He does not pay off on the first or fifteenth of the month. But He promises that He will reward you for any good thing you do on your job. You will come to a place in your life when you have staked your job, your security, and even your future on what God has said. What a commitment! What a witness! What courage! In the confidence that God can be trusted, even with your job, you have remembered the workday and kept it holy.[8]

Whatever form your conclusion takes, there are several other things to keep in mind. Don't introduce new material in the conclusion. These final moments should drive home what you have said, and they should not take the audience off into new avenues of thought. A sermon moves the guns into position. Now is the

---

8. For an extended discussion of visualization, see Alan H. Monroe, *Principles and Types of Speech*, pp. 327–29.

time to fire the shot at the listener's mind and emotions. Spend these important moments driving home the central idea of your sermon.

Do not tell your congregation that you intend to conclude and then fail to do so. Unfortunately, words such as "finally" or "in conclusion" sometimes promise what they don't deliver. In fact, words such as these should be used sparingly. In a well-planned sermon, conclusions should conclude without announcing their appearance.

Your conclusions need not be long. At times a sudden stop can have powerful effect. You will find your strongest conclusions are those that stop a sentence or two before the audience expects it. Poorly prepared conclusions that wander about looking for an exit line leave a congregation looking toward the exit. In the words of an old farmer, "When you're through pumpin', let go of the handle." William E. Sangster puts it clearly:

> Having come to the end, stop. Do not cruise about looking for a spot to land, like some weary swimmer coming in from the sea and splashing about until he can find a shelving beach up which to walk. Come right in, and land at once. Finish what you have to say and end at the same time. If the last phrase can have some quality of crisp memorableness, all the better, but do not grope even for that. Let your sermon have the quality that Charles Wesley coveted for his whole life: let the work and the course end together.[9]

---

9. William E. Sangster, *The Craft of Sermon Construction*, p. 150.

New Concepts

Introduction
Major characteristics of an effective introduction
Conclusion

Definitions

Conclusion—gives the congregation a view of the idea, entire and complete. It brings the central concept to a burning focus and drives home its truth to the minds and lives of the listeners.

Introduction—exposes the congregation to the subject, major idea, or first point of the sermon.

Major characteristics of an effective introduction—
- commands attention for the idea
- uncovers need
- orients the congregation to the body of the sermon and its development

nine

THE DRESS
of Thought

The preacher of Ecclesiastes waited until his conclusion to write down his credentials: "Not only was the Teacher wise," he says with unsettling candor, "but also he imparted knowledge to the people. He pondered and searched out and set in order many proverbs. The Teacher searched to find just the right words, and what he wrote was upright and true" (Eccles. 12:9–10 NIV). To impart his knowledge and to come up with just the right words, the ancient preacher evidently wrote a manuscript.

Not all preachers write out their sermons, nor do preachers who write out sermons write out every sermon, but the discipline of preparing a manuscript improves preaching. Writing scrapes the fungus off our thought, arranges our ideas in order, and underlines the important ideas. "Writing," said Francis Bacon, "makes an exact man exact in thought and in speech." An expository preacher professing a high view of inspiration should respect the power of words. To affirm that the individual words of Scripture must be God-breathed, but then to ignore our own choice of language smacks of gross inconsistency. Our theology, if not our common sense, should tell us that ideas and words cannot be separated. Like Jell-O, concepts assume the mold of the words into which they are poured. As pigments define the artist's picture, so words capture and color the preacher's thought.

The sage of Proverbs compares a word fitly spoken to "apples of gold in settings of silver" (Prov. 25:11). "The difference between the right word and the almost right word," wrote Mark Twain, "is the difference between lightning and the lightning bug." The English poet John Keats was keenly aware of how words shape ideas. One evening as he sat in his study with his friend Leigh Hunt, Hunt read while Keats labored over a poem. At one point, Keats glanced up and asked, "Hunt, what do you think of this? 'A beautiful thing is an unending joy'."

"Good," said Hunt, "but not quite perfect."

There was silence for a while. Then Keats looked up again, "How about this: 'A thing of beauty is an unending joy.'"

"Better," replied his friend, "but still not quite right."

Keats once more bent over his desk, his pen making quiet scratching noises on the paper. Finally he asked, "Now what do you think of this? 'A thing of beauty is a joy forever.'"

"That," said Hunt, "will live as long as the English language is spoken."

Most of the Scriptures that we love best express God's truth in memorable language—Psalm 23, 1 Corinthians 13, Romans 8, John 3:16. Even though Paul disdained eloquence as valuable in itself, he wrote his inspired epistles in inspiring language. While a painting such as Rembrandt's *Christ at Emmaus* can leave us speechless, anyone who generalizes that "a picture is worth a thousand words" has never tried to capture John 3:16, a twenty-five-word sentence with a picture.[1]

1. Kyle Haselden, *The Urgency of Preaching*, p. 26.

There are bright words, as brilliant as a tropical sunrise, and there are drab words, as unattractive as a country bus station. There are hard words that punch like a prize fighter, and weak words as insipid as tea made with one dunk of a teabag. There are pillow words that comfort people and steel-cold words that threaten them. Some words transplant listeners at least for an instant close to the courts of God, and other words send them to the gutter. We live by words, love by words, pray with words, curse with words, and die for words. Joseph Conrad exaggerated only slightly when he declared, "Give me the right word and the right accent, and I will move the world!"

"But language is not my gift." That is the protest of a one-talented servant in the process of burying his ministry. Gift or not, we must use words, and the only question is whether we will use them poorly or well. If you're willing to work at it, you can become more skillful with them than you are. If you compare yourself with C. S. Lewis, Malcolm Muggeridge, or Philip Yancey, you may feel like declaring bankruptcy. Let those artisans provide an ideal toward which you can move. But in every sermon you can strive to be clear and exact in what you mean.

Our choice of words is called *style*. Everyone possesses style—be it bland, dull, invigorating, precise—but however we handle or mishandle words becomes our style. Style reflects how we think and how we look at life. Style varies with different speakers, and an individual speaker will alter his or her style for different audiences and different occasions. Addressing a high school class, for instance, may demand a different style from what you use in addressing a Sunday morning congregation. The polished wording used in a baccalaureate sermon would sound completely out of place in a small group Bible study.

While rules governing good writing also apply to the sermon manuscript, a sermon is not an essay on its hind legs because what you write serves only as a broad preparation for what you will actually say. Your manuscript is not your final product. Your sermon should not be read to a congregation. Reading usually kills a lively sense of communication. Neither should you try to memorize your manuscript. Not only does memorization place a hefty burden on you if you speak several times a week, but an audience senses when you are reading words off the wall of your mind. Agonize with thought and words at your desk, and what you write will be internalized. Rehearse several times aloud without your manuscript. Make no conscious effort to recall your exact wording. Simply try to get your flow of thought clearly in mind. When you step into the pulpit, your written text will have done its work to shape your use of language. Much of your wording will come back to you as you preach, but not all. In the heat of your delivery, your sentence structure will change. New phrases will occur to you, and your speech will sparkle like spontaneous conversation. Your manuscript, therefore, contributes to the thought and wording of your sermon, but it does not determine it.

Writing a sermon differs from writing an essay or a book. Write as though you were talking with someone, and as in conversation, strive for immediate understanding. Authors know that their readers need not grasp an idea instantly. Readers can examine a page at leisure, reflect on what they have read, argue with the ideas, and move along at any rate they find comfortable. Should they stumble across an unfamiliar word, they can get up and consult a dictionary. If they lose a writer's path of thought, they can retrace it. In short, readers control the experience. Listeners, on the other hand, cannot afford the luxury of leisurely reflection. They cannot go back to listen a second time. If they do not take in what is said as it is said, they will miss it completely. Should they take time out to review the speaker's argument, they will miss what the speaker is saying now. Listeners sit at the mercy of the preacher. Speakers, unlike writers, must make themselves understood instantly.

STRONG TRANSITIONS

There are several techniques that can help you think with fierceness and communicate with clarity. Try indenting and labeling your manuscript according to your outline. For example, the material that you would have under a Roman numeral is flush with the margin. The supporting material for that point would be indented. By doing this, you will imprint on your mind the coordination and subordination of the ideas in your sermon. Listeners, of course, do not hear an outline. They hear a sermon. The outline and the manuscript are for your benefit.

In addition, because transitions carry a heavy burden in spoken communication, they take up more space in a sermon manuscript. Listeners hear your sermon only as a series of sentences. Transitions serve as road signs to point out where the sermon has been and where it is going. Transitions, therefore, are longer and more detailed than in writing.

It is hard to overestimate the importance of clear transitions for clear communication. Major transitions will appear between the introduction and the first major point, and then between the major points within the sermon, and between the body of the sermon and the conclusion. Strong transitions will usually review the major points already covered and show the listener how the points relate to the major idea and to each other, and then they introduce the next point. As a result, major transitions can take up to a paragraph or more in the sermon manuscript.

Minor transitions that link sub-points together may be shorter: sometimes a single word *(therefore, besides, yet, consequently)*, at other places a phrase *(in addition to that, what is more, as a result of this)*, and even more often a sentence or two. Although a writer may imply transitions, a speaker must develop them. It is important to state your point, restate it "in other words," even restate it again, and then repeat it. Clear, full, definite transitions look clumsy on paper, but they run easily in a sermon, and they enable your congregation to think your thoughts with you. A major reason that sermons fail to be clear is that the transitions have not been well crafted.

A CLEAR STYLE

What characteristics of style should you try to cultivate? First of all, you must be clear. Talleyrand once remarked that language was invented to conceal, not reveal the thoughts of men and women. Educated people sometimes speak as though Talleyrand had been their speech instructor. They attempt to impress their audience with the profundity of their thought through the obscurity of their language. A sermon is not deep because it is muddy. Whatever has been thought through can be stated simply and clearly. Poincaré, the brilliant French mathematician, insisted, "No man knows anything about higher mathematics until he can explain it clearly to the man on the street." Similarly, we do not understand a passage from the Bible or a point of theology unless we can express it clearly to the men and women sitting before us.

Make no mistake about it. For preachers, clarity is a moral matter. It is not merely a question of rhetoric, but a matter of life and death. Imagine a physician who prescribes a drug but fails to give clear instruction as to how and when the drug is to be used. The physician puts the patient's life at risk. It is a moral matter for a doctor to be clear. So, too, when we proclaim God's truth, we must be clear. If we believe that what we preach either draws people to God or keeps them away from Him, then for God's sake and the people's sake, we must be clear. Helmut Thielicke reminds us that the offense of preaching doesn't come when people do not understand us, but because they understand all too well, or at least they are afraid they will have to understand it.[2]

Imagine a mass meeting in China with a Communist launching a tirade against Christianity. Someone jumps to his feet and shouts, "Jesus is the Messiah!" The audience would be startled, and the Christian would be ejected for disturbing the meeting. But suppose he cried out, "Jesus Christ is God! He is the only Lord, and all who make the system into a god will go to hell, along with their Communist leaders." The objector would risk being torn to pieces by the authorities. Clarity reveals the offense of the gospel. It also provides life and hope.

A Clear Outline

How then can you bring clarity to your sermon? Clear manuscripts develop out of clear outlines. Communication originates

2. Helmut Thielicke, *Encounter with Spurgeon*, trans. John W. Doberstein (Philadelphia: Fortress, 1963; reprint, Grand Rapids: Baker, 1975), p. 34.

in the mind—not in the fingers, not in the mouth, but in the head. Some preachers have jerky minds. While they have stimulating insights, their thought follows no natural sequence, and their zigzag thinking runs listeners to death. After a bewildering half hour trying to keep up with a jerky speaker, hearers will feel that listening to a dull friend comes as a soothing relief, like taking a cat in your lap after trying to hold on to a squirrel. Zigzag thinking can be straightened out only by outlining your overall thought before working on the details. Laboring over an individual paragraph or sentence is pointless unless you know the broad sweep of thought in your sermon. Clear manuscripts and clear sermons develop from clear outlines.

Short Sentences

Furthermore, to be clear, keep your sentences short. Rudolph Flesch, in *The Art of Plain Talk*, maintains that clarity increases as sentence-length decreases. According to his formula, a clear writer will average about seventeen or eighteen words to a sentence, and will not allow any sentence to wander on over thirty words.[3] In your sermon manuscript, short sentences keep your thought from tangling and therefore are easier for you to remember. When you deliver your sermon, you will not concern yourself at all with sentence length, just as you do not think about commas, periods, or exclamation points. As you preach, your words tumble out in long, short, or even broken sentences, punctuated by pauses, vocal slides, and variations in pitch, rate, and force. Short sentences in your manuscript serve your mind; they have little to do with your delivery.

Simple Sentence Structure

Keep sentence structures simple. A clearer, more energetic style emerges when you follow the thinking sequence: main subject, main verb, and (where needed) main object. In the jargon of grammarians, concentrate on the independent clause before

---

3. Rudolph Flesch, *The Art of Plain Talk*, pp. 38–39.

adding dependent clauses (an independent clause can stand alone as a complete sentence; a dependent clause cannot). If you start into a sentence without pinning down what you want to emphasize, you may end up stressing insignificant details. If you add too many dependent clauses, you complicate your sentences, and that makes them harder to understand and remember. Generally, style will be clearer if you package one thought in one sentence. For two thoughts, use two sentences. Arthur Schopenhauer scolded the Germans, "If it is an impertinent thing to interrupt another person when he is speaking, it is no less impertinent to interrupt yourself." Complicated sentences have an additional disadvantage: they slow the pace of the sermon. As Henry Ward Beecher put it, "A switch with leaves on it doesn't tingle."

Simple Words

Simple words also contribute to a clear style. Ernest Campbell tells of a wag who, in a moment of frustration, declared, "Every profession is a conspiracy against the layman."[4] Any citizen who has battled with an income tax return wonders why the Internal Revenue Service cannot say what it means. Lawyers assure themselves of a place by embalming the law in legalese. Scientists keep the little person at bay by resorting to symbols and language that only the initiates understand.

Theologians and ministers, too, seem to keep themselves in office by resorting to language that bewilders ordinary mortals. Beware of jargon! Specialized vocabulary helps professionals within a discipline to communicate. But it becomes jargon when it is used unnecessarily or with people who do not understand it. While it takes three years or more to get through seminary, it can take you ten years to get over it. If you pepper your sermons with words like *eschatology, angst, pneumatology, exegesis, existential, Johannine, the Christ-event,* you throw up barriers to communication. Jargon combines the pretentiousness of big words with the

---

4. Ernest T. Campbell, *Locked in a Room with Open Doors* (Waco: Word, 1974), p. 46.

deadness of a cliché, and it is often used to impress rather than to inform an audience.

Use a short word unless you find it absolutely necessary to use a longer word. Josh Billings struck a blow for simplicity and clarity when he said, "Young man, when you search Webster's dictionary to find words big enough to convey your meaning, you can make up your mind you don't mean much." Long words have paralysis in their tails. Legend has it that several decades ago a young copywriter came up with an ad for a new kind of soap: "The alkaline element and fats in this product are blended in such a way as to secure the highest quality of saponification, along with the specific gravity that keeps it on top of the water, relieving the bather of the trouble and annoyance of fishing around for it at the bottom of the tub during his ablution." A more experienced ad-man captured the idea in two simple words: "It floats." George G. Williams estimates that from 70 to 78 percent of the words used by W. Somerset Maugham, Sinclair Lewis, Robert Lewis Stevenson, and Charles Dickens have only one syllable.[5] Seventy-three percent of the words in Psalm 23, seventy-six percent of the words in the Lord's Prayer, and eighty percent of the words in 1 Corinthians 13 are one-syllable words. All the big things in life have little names, such as *life, death, peace, war, dawn, day, night, hope, love, home.* Learn to use small words in a big way.

No matter how accurately a phrase or word expresses a speaker's meaning, it is worthless if the listeners do not know what it means. "Speak," said Abraham Lincoln, "so that the most lowly can understand you and the rest will have no difficulty." Billy Sunday, the noted evangelist, understood the value of simplicity when he said, "If a man were to take a piece of meat and smell it and look disgusted, and his little boy were to say, 'What's the matter with it, Pop?' and he were to say, 'It is undergoing a process of decomposition in the formation of new chemical compounds,' the boy would be all in. But if the father were to say, 'It's rotten,' then the boy would understand and hold his nose.

5. George G. Williams, *Creative Writing for Advanced College Classes*, p. 106.

'Rotten' is a good Anglo-Saxon word, and you do not have to go to a dictionary to find out what it means."[6]

This does not mean that you should talk down to a congregation. Instead, your rule of thumb should be: Don't overestimate your audience's religious vocabulary, or underestimate their intelligence.

A DIRECT AND PERSONAL STYLE

In addition to being clear, a second major characteristic of spoken style is that it must be direct and personal. While an essay is addressed "to whom it may concern," a sermon is delivered to the men and women of the First Presbyterian Church near Ninth and Elm Streets on June 15 at 10:30 in the morning. The writer and the reader sit alone, distant from each other and unknown. Preachers speak to their hearers face to face and call them by name. Written language communicates the results of thinking, while spoken language represents a spontaneity of thought that Donald Bryant and Karl Wallace describe as "the-vivid-realization-of-idea-at-the-moment-of-utterance."[7] Therefore a sermon should not sound like a thesis read to a congregation. It sounds like lively conversation where the speaker is thinking in the act of speaking. The feeling of good preaching is that you are talking to and with your hearers. You are thinking about ideas the instant that you utter them. Both speaker and listener sense they are in touch with each other.

Sermons use direct address. While a writer may say, "In their conversations, Christians must be careful of how they speak about others," a preacher will more likely say, "You must be careful of how you talk about others." The personal pronoun *you* gives both minister and audience a sense of oneness. While *you* can be effective, at other times you will say *we* because you mean *you and I*. Though the *we* of direct address stands in contrast to the editorial *we* that substitutes for the pronoun *I*, an editorial *we* sounds as though the preacher were speaking for a committee.

6. John Pelsma, *Essentials of Speech*, p. 193.
7. Donald C. Bryant and Karl R. Wallace, *Fundamentals of Public Speaking*, p. 129.

The *we* of oral style, like the *we* in good conversation, means *you and I* together.

Speakers will use questions where writers may not. A question invites the listener to think about what the preacher will say next, and often is used in a transition to introduce a major point or a new idea. Questions are sometimes employed in the conclusion of a sermon. Questions show clearly that the audience and speaker are face-to-face. Good questions provoke thought and help listeners anticipate what will come next.

Personal style pays little attention to the conventions of formal writing. Public speakers use contractions (such as *can't, we'll, wouldn't*) and often split infinitives (such as *to deeply disapprove*). Any speech appropriate in lively conversation fits preaching. This doesn't mean, of course, that anything goes. Poor grammar, gutter language, or faulty pronunciations may unsettle listeners, and like a giggle in a prayer meeting, all of these raise doubts about a preacher's competence.

What about the use of slang? It gets mixed reviews. When it is used deliberately, slang can capture attention and inject a sense of casualness and informality into the sermon. When it is used thoughtlessly, slang sounds trite and even cheap, and it betrays a lazy mind. Personal, direct speech does not call for careless use of language or inappropriate or undignified English. The language of effective preaching should be the language of stimulating conversation between thoughtful people.

A VIVID STYLE

Vividness is a third characteristic of effective style. Wayne Minnick argues that communication that taps into a listener's experience appeals to both mind and feelings. We learn about the world around us through hearing, sight, smell, taste, and touch. To get your listeners to experience your message, therefore, you must appeal to their senses.[8] You do this directly through both sight and sound. Your congregation sees your gestures and facial expressions and hears what you say. You also

8. Wayne C. Minnick, *The Art of Persuasion*, chap. 7.

stimulate the senses indirectly through your use of words. Language helps listeners recall impressions of past experiences and, to some degree, they respond to the words as they did to the events. For example, gastric juices may flow when we hear the words *hot buttered bread*, and then stop in a shudder if we think of roaches crawling on it. Your words cause people to connect with new experiences out of feelings about past experiences.

Your vividness increases when you use specific, concrete details and plenty of them. We label a phrase *specific* when it is explicit and exact, and *concrete* if it paints a picture on the mind. The figure $1,923,212.92 is specific down to the penny, but it is not concrete. The figure $275 on your monthly electric bill is concrete. While you can't visualize the first figure, you can the second. Specific details add interest if they are concrete. They communicate because they relate to the experiences of the audience. Therefore, instead of *produce*, say *cabbages, cucumbers, carrots, and oranges.* Rather than *weapon*, talk about a *heavy lead pipe.* Instead of *major cities,* be specific: *New York, Chicago, Dallas, San Francisco.* The following statement is abstract: "In the course of human experience, we observe that the events of our existence have definite cyclical characteristics. Awareness of this will direct observers to a high degree of appropriateness in their actions." The preacher in Ecclesiastes expressed that same thought this way: "For everything there is a season, and a time for every purpose under heaven: a time to be born, and a time to die; . . . a time to weep, and a time to laugh; a time to mourn, and a time to dance; . . . a time to keep silence, and a time to speak" (Eccles. 3:1–7 ASV).

Like an artist or a novelist, you must learn to think in pictures. That means you must visualize details. Gustave Flaubert gave his writing disciple, Guy de Maupassant, an assignment: "Go down to the [railroad station] and you will find there about fifty cabs. They all look pretty much alike, but they are not alike. You pick out one and describe it so accurately that when it goes past, I cannot possibly mistake it."[9]

9. Christian Gauss, *The Papers of Christian Gauss,* ed. Katherine Gauss Jackson and Hiram Haydn (New York: Random House, 1957), p. 145.

Your speech will become more vivid if you let nouns and verbs carry your meaning. Adjectives and adverbs clutter speech, and they keep company with weak nouns and verbs. According to E. B. White, "The adjective hasn't been built that can pull a weak or inaccurate noun out of a tight place." Strong nouns and verbs stand alone. *A tall man*, should become *a giant*; a *large bird* should become *a pelican* or *an eagle* or *a vulture*. Say *he bellowed*, not *he talked very loudly*; or *he trotted* rather than *he went quickly*. Be especially careful of qualifiers like *very, so, quite, rather, too*. They betray our failure to choose words of substance.

Scalding has a strength that *very hot* does not; *excruciating* hurts more than *too painful*; and *scintillating* paints a better picture than *so interesting*. When choosing your verbs, use live ones. Finite, active verbs make a sentence go. The principle to follow is "somebody does something." Too many passive verbs suck the life out of speech: *opinions and judgments are formed by us on the basis of what we have known* sounds dead. *We think as we have known* possesses vitality. *A good time was had by all* lies there while *everyone had a good time* moves.

Verbs, like nouns, wake up the imagination when they are precise. *She went* gets her there, but not as clearly as *crawled, stumbled, shuffled, lurched*. He *shouts, shrieks, rants, whispers* tell us what *says* does not say.

Your vividness also increases when you employ fresh figures of speech. Metaphors and similes produce sensations in listeners and cause them to recall images of past experiences. Alexander Maclaren stimulates the sense of touch when he says, "All sin is linked together in a slimy tangle like a field of seaweed so that a man, once caught in its oozy fingers, is almost sure to drown." Lord Byron appeals to sight when he tells us:

> The Assyrian came down like a wolf on the fold,
> And his cohorts all gleaming in silver and gold.

Charles H. Spurgeon captured the senses in a simile that refers to a past era: "The great universe lay in the mind of God like unborn forests in the acorn's cup." Alfred North Whitehead touched on sight and smell when he reflected, "Knowledge doesn't keep any better than fish." Figures of speech conserve time by packing more into a phrase than word-wasting speakers express in a paragraph. Consider a few:

Fig-leaf phrases that cover naked ignorance

Words that have been hollowed out on the inside and filled with whipped cream

Cliches that stand like tombstones over dead ideas

If Protestantism is found dead, the sermon will be the dagger in her heart.

He avoided the sticky issues as though he were stepping around puddles of hot tar.

Metaphors and similes, like lobsters, must be served fresh. Both the literal and figurative meanings should strike the mind of the listener at the same instant. When the literal image fades because the comparison has been overworked, the figure loses its force. Hearers become tone-deaf to them. The following that once may have hit like a one-two punch now hardly reach the chin:

Outreach of the church

Tried and true

Lost and dying world

Born-again Christians

Throw the baby out with the bathwater

Souls for your hire

A prayer-hearing and prayer-answering God

Straddle the fence

Sharing

Fellowship

When a comparison has turned stale, toss it out and come up with a fresh one that clarifies your point and keeps your audience alert. Relevance shows up in style as well as content. While we speak the eternal message, it must be in today's words. Study magazine ads or radio or television commercials for easily understood language that speaks to the inhabitants of our culture. Common observation tells us what linguistic tests have proved— much of the language used in our pulpits is "imprecise, irrelevant, and insignificant."[10]

Effective style cannot be taught like a mathematical formula. Mastery of "the well-dressed word" requires an eye for particulars and a search for significant resemblances between things not ordinarily associated with one another. In short, doing away with hackneyed and tired speech demands your imagination. In expository preaching, nothing has been more needed—or more lacking. Expositors who represent the creative God dare not become, in Robert Browning's description, "clods untouched by a spark."

How can you shun the sin of boring people?

1. *Pay attention to your own use of language.* In private conversation, don't shift your mind into neutral, using phrases that idle rather than move. Cultivate fresh comparisons in ordinary conversation and you will find them easier to use when you preach. Beecher gave this testimony about illustrations, which also applies to style: ". . . while illustrations are as natural to me as breathing, I use fifty now to one in the early years of my ministry. . . . I developed a tendency that was latent in me, and educated myself in that respect; and that, too, by study and practice, by hard thought, and by a great many trials, both with the pen, and extemporaneously by myself, when I was walking here and there."[11]

2. *Study how others use language.* When writers or speakers shake you awake, examine how they did it. Because poetry bursts with similes and metaphors, studying verse develops a feel for figurative language. *Reader's Digest* has a regular feature called "More Picturesque Speech" that offers similes and metaphors that are alive and compelling.

10. Donald O. Soper, *The Advocacy of the Gospel* (New York: Abingdon, 1961), p. 36.
11. Henry Ward Beecher, *Yale Lectures on Preaching*, p. 175.

3. *Read aloud.* Reading aloud does two things for you. First, your vocabulary will increase. As youngsters, we learned to speak by listening and imitating long before we could read or write. Reading aloud recreates that experience. Second, as you read aloud a style better than your own, new patterns of speech and creative wording will be etched on your mind. You will develop a feel for picture-making language. Read to your spouse and children so that you'll be forced to interpret what you read. Read novels, plays, sermons, and especially the Bible. The King James Version presents God's truth in Shakespearean grandeur, and the New International Version puts it into more up-to-date dress. Both have impressive style.

New Concepts

Style
Characteristics of effective sermon style:
    Clear
    Direct and personal
    Vivid

Definition

Style—the choice of words.

ten

HOW TO PREACH
So People Will Listen

Most books on preaching say a great deal about the development of the sermon but little about its delivery. That is reflected in the way we preach. While ministers spend hours every week on sermon construction, they seldom give even a few hours a year to thinking about their delivery. Yet sermons do not come into the world as outlines or manuscripts. They live only when they are preached. A sermon ineptly delivered arrives stillborn.

The effectiveness of our sermons depends on two factors: what we say and how we say it. Both are important. Apart from life-related, biblical content, we have nothing worth communicating; but without skillful delivery, we will not get that content across to a congregation. In order of significance, the ingredients making up the sermon are thought, arrangement, language,

201

voice, and gesture. In priority of impressions, however, the order is reversed. Gestures and voice emerge as the most obvious and determinative part of preaching. Every empirical study of delivery and its effect on the outcome of a speech or sermon arrives at an identical conclusion: your delivery matters a great deal.[1]

Not only do your voice and gestures strike the audience's senses first, but your inflections and actions transmit your feelings and attitudes more accurately than your words. Scholars in several disciplines—psychology, anthropology, sociology, and speech communication, to name a few—investigated the effects of nonverbal communication. These researchers observed how we broadcast messages by the way we sit or stand, by our facial expressions, by our gestures, and even by how much space we allow between ourselves and those we meet.[2] As a by-product of these studies, several paperbacks promised to interpret our silent language so that readers could use it to personal advantage. The overclaim of these books produced as many skeptics as believers. Individual and cultural differences in nonverbal communication make dogmatic assertions about the meaning of body language simplistic and possibly dangerous. For example, to assert that arms folded across the chest always reveals that an individual wants to shut out those around her is like saying that the word *model* always refers to a small-scale replica of a large object. The context means more than the action.

Yet no observant person would seriously deny that we communicate messages even when we do not speak. Friends believe that one measure of the depth of their relationship lies in their ability to understand each other even when they sit together quietly. We determine that, right or wrong, casual acquaintances or even strangers are friendly, angry, or worried by reacting to their

1. Wayne N. Thompson, *Quantitative Research in Public Address and Communication,* p. 83.

2. See, for example, *Journal of Communication* 22 (1972): 335–476. This entire issue (no. 4) deals with nonverbal communication; individual articles on the subject appear in this journal regularly. Also see Robert Rosenthal et al., "Body Talk and Tone of Voice: The Language without Words," *Psychology Today* 8 (September 1974): 64–68; and Ernst G. Beier, "Nonverbal Communication: How We Send Emotional Messages," *Psychology Today* 8 (October 1974): 53–56.

posture, facial expressions or tone of voice. Smiles, frowns, stares, winks, eye contact, or glances affect whether we like, dislike, trust, or distrust those we meet. The writer of Proverbs underscored the power of nonverbal communication when he observed, "A worthless person, a wicked man, is one who walks with a perverse mouth, who winks with his eyes, who signals with his feet, who points with his fingers; who with perversity in his heart devises evil continually, who spreads strife" (Prov. 6:12–14 NASB). The eyes, hands, face, and feet say as much to a congregation as the words we utter—in fact, more. In a famous study, psychologist Albert Mehrabian broke it down to a formula. Only seven percent of a speaker's message comes through his words; thirty-eight percent springs from his voice; fifty-five percent comes from his facial expressions.[3]

This research relates to preachers and preaching. First, our nonverbal language has strategic importance in public speaking. When we address a congregation, three different communication networks operate at the same time: our words, our intonation, and our gestures. All three communicate ideas. When actor George Arliss first read the play *Disraeli*, he advised the author to take out two pages: "I can say that with a look," he said. "What look?" asked the author. Arliss demonstrated, and the pages came out.[4] In fact, our actions may often be more expressive than our words. To place the finger on the lips says more than "Be quiet." Opening our eyes and raising our eyebrows expresses surprise better than words, and a shrug of the shoulders communicates an idea beyond what we say. In general, nonverbal elements more frequently communicate emotions and attitudes. Edward T. Hall sums up the finding of social scientists when he observes, "In addition to what we say with our verbal language, we are constantly communicating our real feelings in our silent language—the language of behavior."[5]

Second, both research and experience agree that if nonverbal messages contradict the verbal, listeners will more likely believe

3. Flora Davis, "How to Read Body Language," in *The Rhetoric of Non-Verbal Communication: Readings*.

4. Lauren Reid, *Speaking Well*, p. 141.

5. Edward T. Hall, *The Silent Language*, p. 10.

the silent language. It seems more difficult to lie with the whole body than with the lips alone. This is the thrust of Sigmund Freud's observation: "No mortal can keep a secret. If his lips are silent, he chatters with his fingertips; betrayal oozes out of him at every pore." Your words may insist "This is important," but if your voice sounds flat and expressionless and your body stands limp, the congregation will not believe you. If you shake your fist at your hearers while you say in scolding tones, "What this church needs is more love and deep concern for one another!" the people in the pew will wonder whether you know about the love you are talking about. Because a vast amount of our preaching involves attitudes that either reinforce or contradict what our words proclaim, we dare not ignore delivery.

A third observation about effective delivery is that it begins with desires. The philosopher-humorist Abe Martin suggests, "There is more difference between a professional and an amateur than anything else on earth." In public speaking, the amateur says words; the professional, on the other hand, possesses a deep desire to communicate. Amateurs settle for getting their ideas out of their heads, while professionals strive to get ideas into our heads. In the preacher, technical knowledge and training in the art of public address cannot take the place of conviction and responsibility. Having something to say to a congregation that you want them to understand and live by provides an essential stimulus for effective delivery. It produces the emotional "set" for speaking. We are not merely reciting a script. We are communicating ideas that matter to us.

When we concentrate on ideas, with the desire to make listeners understand and accept them, strong delivery comes naturally. It does not emerge from slavishly following a set of rules. Charles R. Brown, in his Yale Lectures on Preaching, described the pulpit work of George Macdonald in London:

> He read for the Scripture lesson that morning the eleventh chapter of Hebrews. When the time came for the sermon, he said: "You have all heard about these men of faith. I shall not try to tell you what faith is—there are theological professors who can do that much better than I could do it. I am here to help you believe."

Then followed such a simple, heartfelt, and majestic manifestation of the man's own faith in those unseen realities which are eternal, as to beget faith in the minds and hearts of all his hearers. His heart was in his work, and his delivery was effective because it rested back upon the genuine beauty of his own inner life.[6]

"His heart was in his work." No rules can take the place of that. Sincerity, enthusiasm, and deep earnestness tear down barriers that allow the real person to break free. In that sense, effective delivery approximates the everyday give-and-take of honest conversation.

Saying that pulpit delivery resembles conversation, however, does not mean that our ordinary ways of speaking are necessarily our best ways. How we talk in private develops from an accumulation of lifelong habits. We can acquire poor habits of communication just as we develop bad habits of posture or eating. In addition, some of our behavior that is inconspicuous in private situations becomes distressingly obvious in public speaking. When we address an audience, everything about us becomes enlarged and emphatic. Stuffing hands in the pocket, stroking the hair or face, playing with a ring, fussing with a necktie or a scarf, shuffling with the feet may not be noticed when we're talking with our friends, but they become the bad grammar of delivery. Mannerisms and repetitious behavior peculiar to you may go unnoticed by your friends and be tolerated by your associates, but in the pulpit, they scream for attention and divert your listeners from what you are saying. In the pulpit, therefore, the movement of your body must be disciplined to be effective.

At first, attempts to improve your delivery will feel unnatural. Novices may insist that they should abandon the effort because a minister is not an actor and working on delivery violates their personality. But acquiring any habit usually involves initial self-consciousness. When you first drive an automobile or take up tennis, for example, you feel awkward, and you must learn to control your behavior. After practice and experience, however, your self-consciousness disappears and a new learned behavior

6. Charles R. Brown, *The Art of Preaching*, p. 170.

comes easily. It takes effort and discipline to seem natural before an audience.

What are some nonverbal factors in delivery to which we should give our attention?

GROOMING AND DRESS

When the apostle Paul declared that he would "become all things to all men, that I might by all means save some" (1 Cor. 9:22 NKJV), he established a basic strategy for Christian communication. In matters of moral indifference, what matters most is not your feelings but the feelings and attitudes of others. Because grooming and dress make a difference in how listeners respond to us, they should make a difference to us as well.

A fundamental rule of grooming and dress is that they should fit the audience, the situation, and the speaker. Evolving fashions and hairstyles, beards, sideburns and mustaches, or dress length make absolute rules impossible. If you are aware of your community and its standards, you will not want your clothing or hairstyle to stand in the way of your ministry. In most cases, people will expect that our hair will be combed and our shoes will be shined. Clothing, whatever its style, should be neat.

A program of regular exercise and proper diet can trim off excess pounds that sometimes hinder communication. It is hard to believe that a preacher who is thirty pounds overweight takes seriously the biblical injunctions about self-control. That is particularly true in areas of the country that are health-conscious. Good grooming also includes the use of deodorants, toothpaste, and breath fresheners. While television commercials make bad breath sound worse than cancer, breath odor and body odor nonetheless can be offenses that build walls where we want to build bridges.

How we dress causes others to make judgments about us without their being aware of why they make those responses. Ministers do not prove that they are expository preachers by looking as though they dressed staring into a Greek text instead of a mirror. While we may dress to be comfortable, clothes should make others comfortable with us as well. You need to be aware of the cultural expectations of your community, and then dress appropriately. As a general rule, a public speaker will dress one notch higher than the audience. A woman speaker, for example, may wear a skirt while women in the audience wear slacks or jeans. A male speaker may wear a tie when men in the audience are wearing sport shirts. In most Sunday services, a suit for a man or a woman is appropriate. In liturgical settings where ministers wear robes, then matters of dress are not as important. Alexander Pope, in another connection, gives us some counsel for the selection of our wardrobes. He said,

> Be not the first by whom the new is tried,
> Nor yet the last to cast the old aside.

If you feel somewhat inadequate in selecting the best wardrobe for your budget, put yourself in the hands of an experienced clothier in your area. The counsel of a professional can save you money and turn a liability into an asset. Experienced clothiers can tell you what is clothing fad, what will soon be gone, and what styles will last for several years. Suits should be kept clean and pressed. For men, socks should cover the leg; pockets should not bulge with collections of pens, datebooks, eyeglasses, and a wallet; the shirt should be fresh; and if a tie is worn, it should be neatly tied. Handkerchiefs displayed should not be limp, or if carried in the pocket, should be clean. Women should dress professionally and in good taste. Darker clothes are usually a better choice than brightly colored clothes. Dangling jewelry should be kept at a minimum. Because a woman speaker stands on a platform above her audience, she should also be sure to wear a longer skirt. In the final analysis, dress should not call attention to us, but should help us call attention to the Word of God.

MOVEMENT AND GESTURES

God designed the human body to move. If your congregation wants to look at a statue, they can go to a museum. Even there, however, the most impressive statues are those that appear alive. In most realms, professionals use their whole body. The conductor of a symphony, the concert pianist, the umpire, the actress, and the golfer all put their bodies into what they do. Accomplished speakers, likewise, let their bodies speak for them. Here is the basic principle for movement and gestures: content should motivate movement.

This principle applies in two ways. First, sometimes you need to move. You give up a great advantage if you stand almost motionless before your people and become little more than a talking head that refuses to let your body interact with the message. You need to set your body free to do what your mind and emotions demand. Don't inhibit the physical expressions that accompany vigorous thought. You need to carry over into preaching the same freedom you give to your hands, arms, and head in personal conversation. While some of us gesture more than others, we should not gesture less in the pulpit than we do in private. In fact, when we speak in public, we need to make our gestures larger, more forceful, and deliberate.

Second, that content should motivate movement also means that some speakers should move less. If you pace back and forth, you reveal your uneasiness, and your movement gets in the way of the listeners' concentration. Your actions should be motivated by your content. If they are not, then you are merely discharging nervous energy. While walking back and forth may benefit you, it does nothing for your congregation. If your movement comes from habit, stand still. If it grows out of your content, drop your inhibitions and express it. For example, when you introduce a new point in your sermon, you may take a step or two from where you're standing to show by your movement the transition in thought. When that idea has been developed and you proceed to another, then move back to your original position again. If you want your listeners to relax after you have made a major point, you may step back and pause.

Remember that most movement should reflect the audience's perspective. They read from left to right. Therefore, your movement as you face them must be from right to left. If you want to establish your first major point, make a movement to your right.

A second major point may be enforced by a movement toward the center, a third major point by a movement to your left. If you are describing a map, you will find it helpful to make a turn away from the audience and picture the map as though it were on a screen behind you. In that way, you will be seeing the map in your mind as the audience sees it. Hamlet's instruction to his actors still holds: "Suit the action to the word, the word to the action." And, we might add, suit the actions and the words to the audience.

A particular part of bodily movement is gestures. They relate to speaking as diagrams do to a book. Gestures are for expression and not exhibition, and they communicate in several ways. Your gestures help you to explain and to describe. If you wanted to depict the walls of Babylon, you will do so more effectively if you gesture as you describe them. Think of the following description without gestures, and then with gestures: "Babylon stood as a monument to pagan power. The city was surrounded by an intricate system of double walls; the outer range covered seventeen miles and was strong and wide enough for chariots to pass on top. These massive walls were buttressed by giant defense towers and pierced by eight large gates."

Your gestures emphasize your speech. Contrast saying "this is extremely important" with your hands hanging limply by your side, and then make the same statement with a clenched fist, shaken at the word *extremely*. Your gesture injects vigor into your voice. If you must pound the pulpit, pound it softly, and avoid shaking your finger at your audience. That action scolds your listeners and talks down to them. Make the same gesture with an open hand; it is far less threatening.

Gestures maintain interest and hold attention. A moving object captures the eye more than one at rest. Stand on the sidewalk and notice how quickly you watch a car moving by and hardly notice one parked in the street.

Gestures put you at ease. When your body works to reinforce your ideas, you feel more confident and alert. One way to overcome the tension that you feel when you begin your sermon is to gesture. A large definite gesture or two will direct your nervousness into positive action.

Gestures also help listeners experience what we feel as they identify with us. At a football game fans cringe when their favorite runner falls victim to a crushing tackle; sometimes spectators will actually kick the seat in front of them while watching a crucial field goal. This projective behavior is called *empathy*. In essence, empathy is sympathetic, muscular response in which your listeners, in a limited way, act with you. Because these subliminal actions tap feelings, listeners are more likely to feel what you feel and hopefully what you wish them to feel about your ideas. If you fidget or fail to control your gestures, your actions reflect your discomfort. Your audience may squirm or in some other way empathize with those actions, feeling uncomfortable as well. Who of us has not attended a piano recital and felt our palms get sweaty when a child has forgotten her piece and goes over the same notes again and again? On the other hand, if through your gestures, you can get your congregation to respond and feel in a manner appropriate to your thought and purpose—even though this takes place on a subconscious level—you increase the likelihood of winning a positive hearing for your message.[7]

Here are four characteristics of expressive gestures:

Spontaneous Gestures

First, your gestures should be spontaneous. Gesture but don't "make gestures." Your gestures should develop from within you as the outgrowth of conviction and feeling. While you can practice gestures, do not plan them. If in preaching the sermon you use gestures that don't come naturally, let them go.

Definite Gestures

Second, your gestures should also be definite. When you make a gesture, make it. A halfhearted gesture communicates nothing positive. Put your body behind it. A simple gesture with the index finger or the open hand involves not only the finger, the

7. See Jon Eisenson and Paul H. Boase, *Basic Speech*, pp. 334–35.

hand and wrist, but the upper arm, shoulder, and back as well. You will even shift your weight slightly for added force. If your gesture appears awkward, it is usually because your entire body doesn't support it.

Varied Gestures

Your gestures should be varied. Repetition of a single gesture, even a spontaneous and forceful one, calls attention to itself and irritates the audience. For instance, a pump-handle gesture gains emphasis, but when it is used too often, it looks as though it needs a well. Stand in front of your mirror and note how many different ways you can use your body. Someone who has bothered to count them insists that we can produce seven hundred thousand distinct elementary signs with our arms, wrists, hands, and fingers.[8] Try using either hand, both hands, an open hand, a closed hand, palm up, palm down. Experiment with your arms, head, eyes, and face. When you get into the pulpit, your practice will be reflected in better gestures.

Properly Timed Gestures

Finally, your gestures should be properly timed. A good gesture either accompanies or precedes the word or phrase that carries most of your meaning. If the stroke of the gesture follows the word or phrase, it looks ridiculous. Poorly timed gestures usually reflect a lack of spontaneity and proper motivation. Planning your gestures before you speak often results in gestures that are poorly timed.

EYE CONTACT

Eye contact probably ranks as the single most effective means of nonverbal communication at your disposal. Eyes communicate. They supply feedback to you, and at the same time, hold

---

8. Richard Paget, *Human Speech: Some Observations, Experiments, and Conclusions as to the Nature, Origin, Purpose, and Possible Improvement of Human Speech.*

your audience's attention. When you look directly at your hearers, you pick up cues that tell you whether they understand what you are saying, whether they are interested, and whether they enjoy the sermon enough to continue listening. As an alert speaker, you will adjust what you say—for example, adding explanation or illustrations—as you interpret those responses. Moreover, when you look listeners in the eye, they feel that you want to talk with them personally. Therefore, pastors who gaze over their audiences' heads, read a manuscript, stare down at notes, look out of windows, or worse, shut their eyes while they speak, place themselves at a crippling disadvantage. Almost without exception, a congregation will not listen attentively to speakers who do not look at them. It is also significant that men and women mistrust someone who avoids eye contact, and as a result, they undervalue what that person says.

Even though you address a congregation as a group, you talk with them as individuals. As you stand to speak, pause and establish personal contact with your listeners. Move your eyes over the congregation, and let them rest for an instant on several different people. Throughout the sermon, continue making eye contact. Talk with one listener at a time for a second or two. Look that person in the eye, then look at someone else. Choose listeners in every section of the sanctuary, and keep eye contact long enough so that they know that you have singled them out for an instant and are speaking to them. If your congregation is very large, then select a small group in one area and look at them for a moment or two, then shift to another group and continue to do that throughout your sermon. Be sure not only to look at your listeners, but to talk with them. Concentrate on communicating with each one the message you want the entire group to understand.

Because facial expression is very important, your people need to see your face. Therefore illuminate the pulpit with a strong light, placed at an angle that keeps your eyes from being thrown into shadow. Take a light meter and test the focus of light in the front of your church. The brightest light should be on the pulpit. Sunday after Sunday preachers stand in dimly lit pulpits and congregations have only a shadowy view of their facial expressions. If you must use a pulpit, it should be located as close to the listeners as possible, at an angle that makes it easy for them to see your eyes and your full range of emotions playing across your face.

VOCAL DELIVERY

Speech consists of more than words and sentences. Your voice conveys ideas and feelings apart from words. Listeners make judgments about your physical and emotional state—whether you are frightened, angry, fatigued, sick, happy, confident—based on the tremor of your voice, its loudness, rate, and pitch. Because your voice is a major tool in your profession, you should understand how your vocal mechanism works, and how to use it skillfully.

The human voice is produced in somewhat the same manner as sound is produced by a wind instrument (see figure 3). Just as the reed in the instrument must vibrate, so must the vocal folds in the larynx, when air is expelled from the lungs. Voice begins, therefore, when a column of air is pumped from the lungs through the bronchial tubes, which connect the lungs to the windpipe. As the exhaled breath moves across the vocal cords in the larynx, located in the upper end of the windpipe, it sets up vibrations that become sound waves. This sound is then amplified as it vibrates in the larynx, throat, sinuses, and mouth. These cavities, called resonators, act somewhat like the hollow section or soundboard of a stringed musical instrument. They increase the volume of sound made by the strings. As the resonating cavities change shape through the movement of the palate, jaws, teeth, lips, tongue, and the back wall of the pharynx, they produce the ultimate quality of the voice. Consonants, such as *l, p, t, d, s, r,* are also formed as these movements take place.[9]

Even this casual understanding of the vocal mechanism reveals that because tone is produced on the exhaled stream of breath, a good supply of breath, steadily controlled, is essential.

9. For an extended discussion of the physiological basis of speech, see Giles W. Gray and Claude M. Wise, *The Bases of Speech*, pp. 135–99.

Figure 3

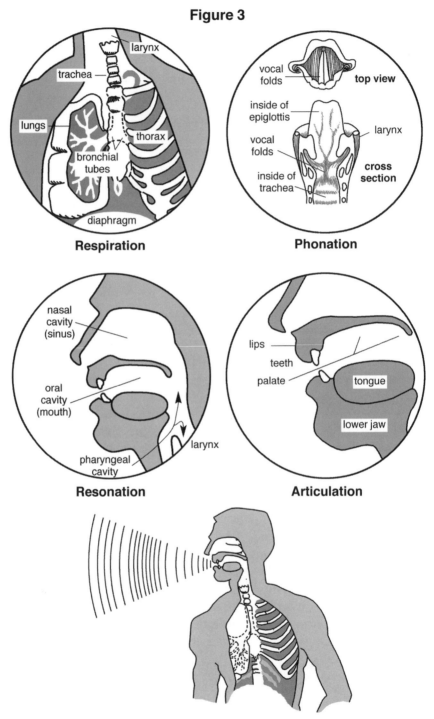

Taken from *Improving Your Speech* by John A. Grasham and Glenn G. Gooder (New York: Harcourt, Brace and World, 1960), pp. 14–15.

Because tone begins with the vibration of the vocal cords, a vocal cord impulse free from undue strain or tension is also necessary. Since the final sound results from modification in the resonating cavities, attention should be given to the throat, mouth, and nasal resonators. You can improve the quality of your voice, even without extended drills, if you understand how vocal sounds are made. For instance, to breathe efficiently, you should expand the belt line instead of the chest. You should be able to recite the entire alphabet on a single breath. Some speakers allow the pitch of their voices to rise when they increase their volume. That can put a strain on your vocal mechanism. Practice going down in your pitch when you go up in force. Not only does that lead to a more powerful delivery, but it will preserve your voice for years.

Other speakers muffle their sound by speaking with a tight jaw, a lazy tongue, or clenched teeth. Open your mouth when you speak. Open it wide. Other speakers allow too much air to escape as they talk, giving their voice a breathy quality. Some ministers speak too rapidly and slur their words, while others speak in a monotone. Most basic texts on speech supply exercises that can correct these common faults.[10] Major universities and many smaller colleges maintain speech clinics, staffed by competent instructors who can help speakers with more complex problems. With such assistance available, we have little excuse for not optimizing the capability of our voices.

Writers have many different ways to emphasize what they write. They can use exclamation points, commas, question marks, underlining, italics, indentations, and boldface type. Speakers, on the other hand, emphasize what they say in only four ways—by a variety in pitch, punch, progress, and pause. The use of these or a combination of them becomes the punctuation of speech. It is a variety of these elements that makes delivery interesting.

10. See, for example, Alan H. Monroe and Douglas Ehninger, *Principles and Types of Speech Communication*, pp. 203–23.

Pitch

Pitch involves the movement of the voice up and down the scale, in different registers, with various inflections. Sometimes changes in pitch are called *melody*. If someone asks, with an inflection rising rapidly from low to high pitch, "Do you believe in hell?" he is asking a question. Precisely that same sentence, with a different progression in pitch, can imply: "You don't say that you—you of all people—would be so out of touch with modern theology as to believe a medieval superstition like that!" If the individual responded with abrupt downward steps, "I do not," that melody communicates, "No, I don't hold that position. Certainly not! Don't accuse me of such idiocy." While the words themselves don't express disgust, the pitch does.

Monopitch drones us to sleep or wears upon us like a child pounding on the same note on the piano. Failure to control pitch effectively is sometimes the reason that humor falls flat. Listeners cannot tell from our pitch that we are joking.

Punch

Variations in punch or loudness can achieve both interest and emphasis. A change in volume communicates the relative importance of ideas. In the declaration, "The Lord is my shepherd," there are only five words; yet if you repeat that sentence five times and each time you punch a different word, the meaning changes. Not only words, but parts of the sermon can be underlined in people's thinking if you utter them with great volume.

Unfortunately, some preachers know no other way to emphasize their points, and as a result, their sermons sound like shouting matches. They confuse volume with spiritual power, thinking that God speaks only in the whirlwind. Like monopitch, the monotony of unvarying volume wears on a listener. In past centuries, preachers had to shout in order to be heard. Today, with effective public address systems, shouting is no longer necessary, or even desirable. Emphasis comes through variety. Dropping your voice to a mere whisper can put an idea into italics as effectively as a loud shout. Intensity can be as effective as volume.

Unfortunately many ministers use only one degree of force, whereas employing a wide range of volume—ranging from loud to soft—could enhance their delivery.

Progress

You can achieve emphasis through changing the progress or rate of your delivery. For example, speak David's words of grief over the death of his rebellious son Absalom, at the same rate: "Absalom, my son, my son Absalom! Would I had died for thee, O Absalom, my son, my son!" (2 Sam. 18:33 ASV). Then speak the sentences very, very slowly. Then speak the first six words rapidly, with feeling, and the rest of the words slowly. The variety in rate communicates different meanings and emotions.

When you use rate, as in the other means of showing emphasis, the secret lies in variety. As you recite a story, give out facts, or summarize a passage, you usually do so at a lively pace. Then when you come to a key statement or a major point, you slow down so that the congregation will appreciate its importance. The sentences spoken more slowly stand out because they are in strong contrast to the content surrounding them. Your words may also be emphasized by speaking slowly and then speeding up your delivery. But emphasis is more often accomplished by slowing down rather than increasing the rate.

Some speakers have gained a bad reputation for speaking too rapidly, but their problem may be that they fail to vary their rate.

Pause

"By your silence," said Rudyard Kipling, "you shall speak." Skilled speakers recognize that pauses serve as commas, semicolons, periods, and exclamation points. Pauses are the major punctuation marks of speech. Pauses are "thoughtful silences." They go beyond a mere stoppage in speech and give the audience a brief opportunity to think, feel, and respond. The first word or phrase uttered after a pause will stand out from what has preceded it. For even stronger emphasis on a word or phrase, you can pause after the word as well as before it. A pause before the

climax of a story increases suspense, and a dramatic pause introduced when a speaker feels deep emotion can communicate feelings more effectively than words. Pauses not motivated by
thought or feeling, however, confuse listeners just as random
punctuation bewilders a reader.

Many speakers are afraid of silence. They do not have enough
self-control to pause for long. Perhaps they feel they must keep
talking or the audience will think they have forgotten what they
want to say. Rather than pause, therefore, these speakers hurry
on with an unremitting stream of words—or worse, fill their sermons with word whiskers such as *er, and, uh, so, ah.* In some religious circles, the preacher throws in "Amen" and "Praise God"
aimlessly, and these words serve as nothing more than vocalized
pauses. Meaningless sounds and words communicate nothing;
instead they draw attention away from the idea and irritate the
listeners.

A pause will not seem as long to the listener as it does to you.
If you concentrate fiercely on your thought and feel the emotion
of what you are saying, your pause will underline important
points. While you pause, continue to look at your listeners in-
tently. Audiences sense when speakers are thinking hard, and
they will wait with them. There is nothing quite as engaging as
watching someone think on their feet. A few speakers misuse the
technique, and by pausing too long, sound melodramatic. The
pause should be long enough to call attention to the thought, but
not so long that the silence calls attention to the pause.

REHEARSAL

Rehearse your sermon before you deliver it. Put aside your
notes and go through it from memory. Rehearsal tests the structure of your message. The progress of thought that seemed clear
on paper may feel awkward when you actually speak it. As you
speak your sermon, you may change the progression of your ideas
in your manuscript into a pattern that flows more naturally.

Rehearsing also improves your style. As you practice, you may
find a phrase that presents an idea in a particularly effective way.

Don't rehearse in order to memorize the sermon. By all means, feel free to alter words or phrases when you are in the pulpit. You are rehearsing to get a clear progression of thought and to express your thought in language that communicates what you want to say. Practice should not make permanent. It should make you effective.

Rehearsing also improves delivery. Professional actors and actresses would not think of going before an audience without first going over their material orally—usually many times—to be sure that it comes to them easily. They ask, "How can I say this so that it is clear? When should I increase my force, vary my rate, change my pitch, or pause to let a line sink in?" While preachers are more than actors, they should not be less. Effective delivery must be practiced because you cannot think about delivery much as you speak. The good habits acquired in your preparation will come more easily in the pulpit. Beginners profit from rehearsing with a full voice while standing before a mirror or using a tape recorder. More experienced speakers may settle for a *sotto voce* as they mumble through their sermons. For a few, sitting and thinking through their sermons, animated in their imagination by a picture of themselves before their congregations, will be enough. For all of us, having traveled a path before, makes it simpler to follow that path again.

FEEDBACK

Effective speakers look for feedback. They will listen to audiotapes of their sermons, or better still, watch videotapes. It is best to do this several days after you preach when the experience has grown cold. Other pastors invite a selected group of listeners to meet with someone in the church to take thirty minutes to give their reactions to the sermon. They ask simple questions such as: "What do you think the preacher was driving at today?" "Do you think you understood the text from which the minister spoke?" "Were the illustrations helpful?" "Do you have any idea what you may do in the days ahead as a result of the sermon today?" "What is your reaction to the minister's delivery?" "If there were one or two things you could tell the pastor that you think could improve his or her preaching, what would it be?" Let the group meet, turn on a tape recorder, and let them speak freely. Then listen to what they have to say. Usually you will be positively affirmed. People who know you're interested in their reaction will be kind and gentle. At the same time, you can get insight as to what you might do to improve your effectiveness. All of us need all of the help we can get—from God and from the folks who assemble to hear us.

A Final Word

Sometimes when I study the Bible, I get hung up on the details. I know I shouldn't, but I do. Take that incident where Jesus provided supper for about fifteen thousand men, women, and children. All four of the authors who describe Jesus' ministry mention it. They use the event to show us some lofty insights about their Lord. I am ready to get on to those grand lessons, but then John sidetracks me with the detail that it was some nameless youngster who supplied the five rolls and the two small fish Jesus used to perform the miracle. Frankly, I can't get past that kid.

It was a miracle of sorts, wasn't it, that the boy hadn't already devoured his lunch? After all, it was late in the afternoon, and everyone else was getting hungry. Boys I know are always hungry. When I take my grandsons to a ball game, the first thing they want to do is buy a hot dog and soda pop. In fact, they would be content to spend the afternoon at the concession stand eating. Here it is drifting toward evening, and this youngster hadn't touched the lunch his mother made for him that morning.

Perhaps he was too excited to eat. Not much happens in a small community. Villagers take their excitement wherever they can find it. In this case a popular young teacher had come to the area, and He had performed some miracles. He was a happening. Everyone wanted to hear what He would say and to see what He would do. This boy didn't want to miss out on anything that big. He raced to stay ahead of the crowd, to find the best spot up front to catch what was going on. He didn't want to pass half a day looking at some adult's backside.

Maybe the rush and movement kept him from eating his lunch at noon. I have another question: What made him decide to donate his lunch to Jesus? Okay, Andrew asked him for it. But imagine the conversation: "Look, son, the people are hungry and we have to find some way to feed them. Is that your lunch you have there? Would you mind letting Jesus have it? We're trying to scrape up something, anything. Your lunch might help."

Wouldn't any normal kid have responded, "Mister, you're crazy! All I've got is five rolls and a couple of sardines. And I'm getting real hungry myself. I haven't eaten anything since break-fast. This won't even be enough for me. You've been out in the sun too long if you think that what I've got in this bag could feed this crowd." That's what I would have said, wouldn't you?

But for some reason, this lad went along with it. He surren-dered his lunch to Andrew, who in turn sheepishly turned it over to Jesus. "Here is a boy with five small barley loaves and two small fish," he reported, "but how far will they go among so many?"

The answer to that is easy: Not far. Not far at all.

There's something else. When the disciples fed the crowd, how did they manage to get everyone to eat the same menu? Weren't there some people in the crowd who complained about the food? Weren't a number of them picky eaters? Fish and bread isn't everybody's favorite dish. In a gathering that large, there must have been some who had eaten some spoiled fish when they were growing up and couldn't stomach it as adults. Did everyone in the crowd realize how hungry they were, or how desperately they needed to eat something nourishing that afternoon? I know that the text tells us that "everybody had enough," but isn't it possible that some of the basketfuls left over came from people who refused to eat the entrée?

Don't you identify with that youngster and with Andrew? Any preacher does. No one in his right mind who thought about it would ever choose to be a preacher. It's a commitment to the impossible. As I enter the pulpit, I wonder, "How can what I have prepared possibly feed so many?" My best sermons are little more than some fish and chips and at times they are a bit greasy. Isn't it folly to believe that what I have in my hand could possibly meet the hungers of an entire congregation?

> After you give it your best shot,
> When you do the most diligent exegesis you can do,
> When you have read the best commentaries and crafted your sermon with skill and then delivered it with passion,
> Even if you follow all the counsel I have given you in this book,
> Face it: When you have done your utmost, it's simply not enough.
> At best, you have two small fish and five rolls. (All right, if you're really gifted, you may have three fish and an extra roll or two.)
> But you never have enough to feed the multitude.

Only Jesus Christ through His Spirit can do that. You must give your sermon to Him. Preaching is ultimately His work. It's astonishing, sometimes, how He not only multiplies our effort but also creates in listeners a hunger for what we offer them.

Every preacher knows the surprise. The woman who calls you in the middle of the week to thank you for your sermon, "particularly that part about apologizing to your children when you have messed up." You think back through the message and you hadn't preached about that at all. Or you celebrated communion and spoke a brief word about the death and resurrection of Jesus. You learn later that a person in your congregation who had begun an affair broke it off because God had spoken to him that morning. You never had someone like that in mind at all. You get a note, unsigned, that simply says, "Thank you for letting God use you. You'll never know the difference it has made." You wonder how or why or when. Christ has a secret passageway into people's lives that you and I know little about. Give your sermon to Him.

Of course, we will not give God that which costs us nothing. We will give Him our best. Yet, in the final analysis there are no great preachers. There's only a great Christ who does startling things when we place ourselves and our preaching in His hands.

William Barclay, who himself held onto the faith with shaky hands, told about A. J. Gossip, a man "who lived closer to God than any man I have ever known." At one time Gossip was minister of St. Matthew's in Glasgow. There was a week when he went through pressures that every preacher knows that made it impossible for him to prepare as he should. "You know the stair up to the pulpit in St. Matthew's?" Gossip asked. "You know the bend in the stair? Jesus Christ met me there. I saw Him as clearly as I see you. He looked at the sermon in my hand. 'Gossip,' He said to me, 'is this the best you could do for me this week?'" Gossip went on: "Thinking back over the pressures of that week, I could honestly say: 'Yes, Lord, it is my best.'" Then said Gossip: "Jesus Christ took that poor thing that Sunday morning and in his hands it became a trumpet!"[1] It is always so. Even on our best weeks we have only some fish and bread. But we serve the living Lord. Give Him your small lunch and trust Him to feed His people.

---

1. William Barclay, *A Spiritual Autobiography* (Grand Rapids: Eerdmans, 1975), p. 13.

ANSWERS

EXERCISES IN CHAPTER 2

1. Subject: What is the test of a good sermon?
   Complement: It reveals what you are.

2. Subject: Why has the modern pulpit lost its authority?
   Complement: It has ignored the Bible.

3. Subject: How do the young and old differ in their memo-ries and their time?
   Complement: The young have few memories and lots of time while the elderly have lots of memories and little time.

4. Subject: Where does charity start?
   Complement: Where it connects with need.

5. Subject: What should dissatisfied teenagers do?
   Complement: Go it on their own if they think they know
   everything.

6. Subject: Who enters the kingdom of heaven?
   Complement: Those who do the will of the Father.

7. Subject: When should you think about God?
   Complement: While you are still young.

8. Subject: How should we relate to others as we minister to
   them?
   Complement: Treat them as you would members of your
   own family.

9. Subject: What is essential for forgiveness to take place?
   Complement: Sin must be exposed before God.

10. Subject: Who is a blessed person?
    Complement: The honest individual whose sin the Lord
    has forgiven.

EXERCISES IN CHAPTER 4

1. Subject: Why don't older people learn?
   Complement: They feel they already know and are too
   concerned about other matters.
   Functional question being addressed: Is it true? (validity)

2. Subject: How should you listen to the Word of God?
   Complement: Listen carefully and obey.
   Functional question being addressed: So what? What dif-
   ference does it make? (application)

3. Subject: How can you help your golf game in the winter?
   Complement: Practice before a full-length mirror.
   Functional question being addressed: Is it true? (validity)

4. Subject: Why should we love one another?
   Complement: Love fulfills all the demands of the law.
   Functional question being addressed: So what? What difference does it make? (implication)

5. Subject: How do we learn about reality?
   Complement: We learn by repeated, unconscious experience.
   Functional question being addressed: What does it mean? (explanation)

6. Subject: What is the importance of memory in music?
   Complement: Without it we would have no melody.
   Functional question being addressed: What does it mean? (explanation)

7. Subject: How should I live because I only live once?
   Complement: Do good to others now.
   Functional question being addressed: So what? What difference does it make? (implication)

8. Subject: How have play and work lost their traditional distinctions?
   Complement: What was play has been made into work, and what was work is now recreation.
   Functional question being addressed: What does it mean? (explanation)

9. Subject: What is a result of having the law?
   Complement: It prompts us to sin.
   Functional question being addressed: Is that true? (validity)

Appendix 2

SAMPLE SERMON
and Evaluation

Here is a sermon based on Matthew 20:1–16. If you take a look at the passage, you will find that it has its roots in chapter 19, and therefore the chapter division is an unfortunate one. It is not offered as a model sermon, but merely as one that has grown out of the process we have just discussed. It would be wise to take a few moments to read the passage so that you have it in mind. Once you read the sermon we'll look back at it together. We will use it to review what we have discussed in the previous pages. (The paragraphs are numbered in order to refer back to them in the closing discussion.)

"THE GREAT WAGE DISPUTE"

1. Jesus made a wise mid-career adjustment. Until the time He was thirty, He had worked in the firm of "Joseph and Sons

Carpenters" in the town of Nazareth. Then God called him to preach. Many observers feel that the switch of professions was a fortunate one. If He had stayed in business, He would have gone bankrupt.

2. At least that's what many hardheaded business types might feel when they read this account of a labor dispute that Jesus told with obvious approval in Matthew 20:1–16. As a case study on how to handle labor-management relations, it gives a business analyst cold chills.

3. The story starts out sensibly enough. It's harvest season, and early in the morning a grape grower drives into the center of town. He goes to the corner where farmworkers assemble hoping for a day's work, and the grower selects some of these men to pick grapes for him. Before they go out to the vineyard, he signs a contract with them to pay a denarius for the day's work. At the time a glut existed in the labor force and a denarius was a generous wage. The owner didn't have to pay that much, but you can overlook his lack of haggling because the man wasn't very astute about business affairs.

4. Then later at nine o'clock in the morning the owner returned to town and saw some other men standing around waiting for someone to hire them. The owner sent this group, too, into his vineyard, but this time without a contract. He promised only to "do what is right." That would unsettle any union leader. A loose arrangement is no substitute for a contract. But, face it, you have to put up with agreements like that when work is hard to find.

5. At noon and then again at three o'clock the vineyard owner returned, and when he spotted other unemployed workers he sent them into his vineyards to pick the grapes. It's the same deal as before. No contract. Just his assurance that he will do what is right by them.

6. Finally at five in the afternoon as the owner was about to call it a day, he saw some other workers standing on the corner with their tools. He stopped and asked them why they weren't working. "We've been standing here all day waiting for someone to hire us," they explained. So with only an hour left before sundown he sent those workers to pick grapes in his vineyard. I suppose the workers were grateful. After all, any work is better than nothing. Even a small paycheck would put some food on their tables.

7. The problem started an hour later at six when the closing whistle blew. The vineyard owner ordered his foreman to pay the workers. The owner was obviously more eccentric than efficient. He got everything backwards. He insisted that the last fellows hired be paid first and the first hired be paid last. So when the laborers lined up last man first, the foreman paid the crew that had worked only sixty minutes a denarius, a full day's wage. The workers who punched in at three and those who signed on at noon also got paid a denarius. In fact, that was true for those who had worked since nine that morning. Those at the back of the line who had started at sunrise got their expectations up. "Hey, there's a bonus today!"

8. But no. When they finally shuffled up to the pay window and received their pay envelope, it contained the denarius they had agreed on. Tempers flared and they sent their representative to the owner to have it out with him. "Look" he argued, "these last guys you hired worked only an hour, and you made them equal to us. It's not right. We picked those lousy grapes all day in the sweltering heat. It's tough work and our hands and backs are sore. We want to file a grievance. We deserve better. You're guilty of unfair labor practices."

9. I don't know how this incident sits with you, but I suspect you want to grab a picket sign and join the workers' protest. This upside-down system of payment strikes us as grossly unfair—just as it did to the workers and to the audience that first heard the story. (What is going on? Why did Jesus tell this story? What's he driving at?)

10. Well, Jesus certainly didn't offer this parable as a model for how Christians should settle wage disputes in the twenty-first century. Imagine the ruckus the press would set up if an employer tried this today. He couldn't operate. He couldn't get to his office because of the picket lines he would have to cross. If he did pay his workers this way one week, he would learn his lesson the following week. His labor force would be crushed in the five o'clock rush going *to* work. Production would collapse. With workers putting in only an hour a day, the work would never get done. (We had better understand why Jesus told this story. Is He

completely unaware of how business works? Why did He tell a story as crazy as this?)

11. The context gives us a clue to what Jesus is driving at. The parable follows Jesus' response to two different men who wanted to sign a contract with God. The first chap was a wealthy young man (Matt. 19:16–26). He approached Jesus to ask Him to spell out exactly what he had to do to earn eternal life. He figured that he had kept the Ten Commandments, but he wanted to know if Jesus could think of anything else that might be involved to qualify. Jesus knew that this man needed radical surgery so he put His scalpel on the cancer in the man's life: "Sell your possessions and give the money to the poor and you will have treasure in heaven. Then come and follow me." If he wanted a contract, he could have it. But the price was more than the young man was willing to pay. He called the whole thing off. His investments and his bank accounts meant everything to him—more than God, or eternal life, or heaven. That's why this prosperous young man walked away from the deal.

12. The second man who wanted to negotiate a contract was Peter (Matt. 19:25–30). He and the other disciples had overheard the conversation with the wealthy inquirer. As a result, Peter raised a candid question. "Look, we have left everything to follow you; what's in it for us?" Peter's question sounds self-serving, but some time or other most of us get around to asking it. At first when we sign on to follow Jesus we may not bring up the question. But then after we have labored in the heat of the day, we get uneasy. Things happen. "What's the deal?" we ask. "What's in it for us?"

13. Some time or other we all get around to Peter's question. Perhaps you have hit some financial difficulties. You see yourself as a dedicated follower of Jesus. Yet, you have to struggle to make ends meet. Others don't have to struggle with a tight budget. It doesn't seem fair. What's the payoff for your commitment? What's in it for you?

14. Perhaps you wrestle with health problems. You have served Christ with all your strength but now you no longer have any. Your health and strength are gone. You wonder, "Lord, what's happening? I've tried to do Your work. Yet, new Chris-

tians who haven't served as long and faithfully as I have are vibrant and healthy. It's not fair. What's my reward? What's in it for me?"

15. Perhaps you have gone to serve Jesus in another part of the world and have struggled with the anxiety and frustration of coping in a different culture. Other Christians stay at home and live in the luxury of affluent America. You take the pressure on yourself and on your family, but every victory is offset by a setback. You have won some and lost some. So what do you get for your sacrifice? You ask, "What's in it for me?"

16. Or you serve in a church where you feel that people have badly mistreated you and taken advantage of you. You hang on when you want to hang it up. Other Christians seem to thrive in their service. They don't seem to have labored as hard or as long as you, but they are doing well. The question nags at you, "So what do I get out of it?"

17. ("What's in it for us?" There's a bargaining streak in Peter's question. But you have to identify with him. Peter felt that he had good reason to ask the question, "We've given up everything to follow you; what do we get out of it?")

18. Jesus responded with gentleness and grace to Peter's question, "What will there be for us?" He could have made Peter feel guilty.

19. Jesus might have said, "Okay, Peter, let's put it all down where we can look at it. What precisely did you give up? You say you gave up your position as vice president of the Zebedee Fish Company. You gave up a promising career in fish. That's impressive. What else?

20. "That's true, you gave *her* up, too. She was a pretty little thing. She had lovely curves and a beautiful shape. You loved to spend time with her. In fact, you thought you would probably spend your life with her. Yes, we'll put that down, Peter. You turned your back on your boat to follow me."

21. If Peter had compiled a list of things that he had given up to follow Christ, Jesus could have shamed him. They seem trivial. Instead, Jesus assured Peter that he and those like him would be well repaid. In the future when Jesus sets up His kingdom, Peter and his friends would have positions beyond the wildest

dreams of any Galilean fisherman. Whatever anyone had given up to follow Jesus will be repaid a hundred times over in addition to receiving eternal life. For Peter and those like him the best was yet to come. God would never be in their debt.

22. Then Jesus made the statement, "But many who are first will be last, and many who are last will be first" (Matt. 19:30). It's a weird saying. It is so important, though, that Jesus rephrased it again at the end of his story, "So the last will be first and the first will be last" (20:16). What's that all about? It sounds like pious nonsense. "The first shall be last and the last shall be first" doesn't work if you are standing in line at the checkout counter at the supermarket, or waiting in a long line at the airport, or lining up to be served at the bakery where everyone takes a number.

23. Actually it doesn't work any place that I can think of. In our society the first are first and the last are last. That's the way the system works in sports, in government, in education, in business, and in most vineyards. In those realms the last are last and the first are first. But Jesus declares that's not the way it works in His kingdom. In His setup "many who are first will be last and many who are last will be first." (What does it mean? What does it mean in the kingdom to have our order of things reversed? Does it make any sense?)

24. "The first shall be last and the last first" means that Jesus changes the order of things. The reason for this reversal is that God doesn't deal with us on the basis of our merit but on the basis of His goodness. We live with a merit system. The people who arrive first get served first. The people who work more hours make more money. The students who make the best grades go to the top of the class. God doesn't work with that system. He rewards us not on the basis of our merit but on the basis of His goodness. He doesn't give us what we deserve. He gives us more than we deserve. He is always fair, but far better than fair, He is always good.

25. Look at what this story shows us. To be allowed to go to work in His vineyard reflects God's goodness. Service in itself is an undeserved reward. Those men standing idle in the square before sundown were not the "idle rich." They were "the idle poor." Unemployment ran high in the country. Work was hard

to find. Their pathetic explanation tells us why they were standing there. "Because no one would hire us." That means, "No one wants us" or "no one needs us." If you have ever spent days or weeks desperately looking for a job, you know that it's more exhausting standing on an unemployment line than working on an assembly line.

26. I have a friend in his early fifties who lost his job when his company downsized. For weeks that man scoured the city trying to find another position. He was willing to take almost any job available, but no firm was interested. It almost killed him. In fact, he grew so depressed that he contemplated suicide.

27. If when you get out of bed in the morning you have meaningful work to do, instead of resenting the alarm clock, breathe a prayer of thanks that you have a job to go to. It is terrifying when a society can't provide employment for someone who wants to work. People seldom crack up under the strain of hard work. They come apart because of meaningless inactivity. The toughest challenge in life is not when you have to work hard. It's when you don't have any work to do at all.

28. Jesus comes to the idle, the unemployed, the lost who have time on their hands and offers us meaningful work to do in His vineyard. That work is in itself a gift. There is fulfillment in serving the Lord of the vineyard. In His work we have a relation with Him and His harvest. The people to be pitied are not the workers in the vineyard, but the idle in the marketplace.

29. Do you doubt that? Compare Peter with that rich young man. Putting aside all the religious jargon for a moment, whose life was better spent? Would you seriously suggest that Peter would have been better off if he could have stayed in the fishing business and become a tycoon? By the standards of their society the wealthy young man was a "first" and Peter was a "last." But don't you feel some sorrow for that young man who turned away from following Jesus and missed out on the timeless life of God? The person to pity is the man or woman who crawls out of bed in the morning, grabs a cup of coffee at the local Starbucks, fights the traffic to the same office, eats at the same restaurant, leaves the same tip, drives home at the same time, watches television, and then falls into bed. He or she retires at sixty-five, plays

golf until seventy-three, and dies with no sense of the eternal about life. Who ends up being first? Who ends up being last?

30. By sending us into the vineyard to work, Jesus delivers us from eternal insignificance. When the Tartar tribes of Central Asia curse their enemies, they don't tell them to "go to hell." Instead they say, "May you do nothing forever." Jesus Christ in His goodness delivers us from that curse. (There is reward just to work in the vineyard, and when it comes to the payoff itself we can count on God's generous goodness to determine our reward.)

31. This parable assures us that our Master is much more than just. He is always that but He is much more than that. He is generous and good. Listen again to the interaction that the owner of the vineyard had with his disgruntled workers (Matt. 19:12–15). They protest that he is unfair. After all, they argue, they had to sweat for twelve hours while some of the other grape pickers had to work for only one. The owner defends himself, "Look, I was not unjust to you. You received everything we agreed on. Certainly you can't argue that I don't have full right over my possessions, can you? I am free to give to the others as much as I gave you." The owner gave unequal treatment, but it was not unjust treatment. He had not wronged the first workers to favor their friends. Those early workers received everything they had agreed on. Everything.

32. The vineyard owner in paying off his workers gave everyone justice. With most of the workers, however, he went beyond what was just. He acted out of the goodness of his heart. Justice forms the background of this story against which goodness appears as goodness and not unfairness. The owner would have been evil if he had cheated those early workers out of what they had bargained for. The emphasis of the parable falls on his magnificent generosity to those eleventh-hour workers. Everyone in the story was treated fairly, but the last men in were also treated with lavish generosity.

33. When you serve Jesus Christ, you don't work for a wage; you receive a reward. In His service you are not rewarded based only on your merit but on His generosity. You are not rewarded on the *quality* of your work—you pick delicious grapes. You are not rewarded on the *quantity* of your work—you pick more

grapes in an hour than the others do in twelve. When you serve Jesus Christ, He does not put you under contract. He puts you under grace.

34. That's how you become a Christian. Salvation is based entirely on God's grace and not on your merit. If you think that you come into a relationship with God based on what you do, you are doomed never to have eternal life at all. That's why the rich man missed it. He couldn't understand that Christ turns our system upside down. He wanted a contract based on his merit, but when he got one, he couldn't handle it. He couldn't get it out of his head that God doesn't work in a system where the first are first and the last last.

35. Peter was inclined to think that after following Jesus everything changed back to the old bookkeeping system. Shouldn't the first who have given up the most have preference over the last? Peter wanted to go back to a wage system. But wages are the wrong way to think about God's dealing with us. The focus of this story is not on how to earn a salary, but on the generous reward of God. It is wrongheaded to bargain with God. We ought to enter into His service with gratitude that we have meaningful work to do and leave the ultimate reward with Him. Jesus wants to treat both the first and last as objects of His generous goodness.

36. (How do you react to the goodness of God?) Most of us are delighted—even thankful—when we sense His bounty in our lives. I suppose those men who worked for an hour and received a full day's pay cheered the owner for his goodness. The test, however, is not how you respond to the goodness of God when it is showered on you, but how you react when you see it displayed to others.

37. The owner asks, "Are you envious because I am good? Do you begrudge me my generosity to others?" In other words he asks, "Are you uptight because I have shown these other workers a measure of generosity they have not deserved? I haven't given you less than you had coming to you, have I? You don't suffer at all because I was openhanded in rewarding these other workers, do you? Are you begrudging me my right to give these other fellows more than they have earned?"

38. We respond, "Of course not, Lord. We're delighted that You are generous to our friends—that's very nice." Yet all the time we are thinking, "Why not me? Why should my friends get to stand around all day when I have to sweat through the heat of the afternoon? Why do other Christians have it easier than I do? When do I get paid?"

39. Isn't it usually when I see God do something out of the ordinary for a close friend or a colleague that I get upset with the way God has dealt with me? It's then I may ignore completely God's goodness in my life, and in my heart I accuse God of being terribly unfair. When I have a contract mentality, that's where I end up.

40. (What is the solution to this attitude? How do I keep from grumbling against the generosity of God? How do I keep from getting upset when God in His goodness allows the last to be first and the first to be last?)

41. The laborers were satisfied as long as they dealt with the owner alone. As long as they focused on the denarius and the work they were given, they were content. It was not until the others showed up and received their pay that the haggling broke out. Then envy set in. Isn't it true that our angry feelings about God's goodness start when we look at the other workers in the vineyard, and decide what God should or should not do in their lives compared to what God has done for us?

42. As long as you concentrate on working for the owner of the vineyard to gather His crop, nothing else matters very much. If you understand He has given you productive work to do and always rewards you out of His generous goodness, you will be satisfied. Realize your Lord doesn't work on the marketplace system that is based on "The first will be first and the last last." His goodness turns that system downside up. "The first shall be last and the last shall be first." Meister Eckhart, the mystic, understood this when he wrote, "The foundation of spiritual blessing is this—the soul looks to the goodness of God with nothing in between."

43. Years ago when our son Torrey was ten or eleven, he came home early one Saturday afternoon from playing with his friends. His mother was frantically trying to get things ready for company that evening. Without being asked, Torrey got out the

vacuum cleaner and vacuumed the whole house. Bonnie told me about it when I got home. I usually paid the kids fifty cents for a job like that. When I asked Torrey what I owed him he replied, "Dad, I just wanted to help." I pulled out my wallet and gave him two dollars. He took it and said, "Dad, I like being in this family. You gave me more than I would have asked for and more than the job was worth!" He honored me more than he knew. Over thirty years have passed since that incident, but I've never forgotten it. How satisfying to have a son who loves you and pitches in and takes your generosity for granted.

Now let's look at the sermon with a series of questions and answers.

WHAT ARE THE SUBJECT, COMPLEMENT, AND EXEGETICAL IDEA OF THE PASSAGE?

Subject: Why is the system of payment reversed in the kingdom of heaven?

Complement: Because God doesn't deal with people on the basis of merit but on the basis of His goodness and generosity.

Idea: In the kingdom of heaven God reverses the human system of wages because He doesn't deal with people on the basis of merit but on the basis of His goodness and generosity.

Exegetical Observation: The parable elaborates on the enigmatic saying in Matthew 19:30, "But many who are first shall be last and the last shall be first." Notice the *for* that opens chapter 20 and tells us that the parable elaborates on that statement. It is the *idea* of the parable.

WHAT IS THE HOMILETICAL IDEA OF THE SERMON?

I played with several statements that I might use:

"God works on an upside-down system of rewards."
"Don't work for God's favor; accept it."
"Work for God, not a wage."

None of these stirred my imagination. I decided, therefore, to go with Jesus' statement, "The first shall be last and the last shall be first." People may have heard that statement because it is occasionally used in common speech, but most would have no idea about where it comes from or what it means. I decided that if I explained the saying, then when listeners heard it again it would bring the theological truth to mind.

WHAT WAS THE PURPOSE FOR PREACHING THIS SERMON?

My purpose was to have listeners respond positively to God's goodness in their own lives and respond to it positively when they witnessed God's goodness in the lives of others.

WHAT IS THE NEED FOR THIS SERMON?

Many Christians feel that God isn't fair. Usually that comes from comparing how God has dealt with them to how God has dealt with others. That leads to envy which rots the soul. Just as the Pharisees were upset when Jesus welcomed sinners, Christians can be upset when God's goodness is shown to others. We can feel that we alone should be the special objects of His generosity.

DID THE SERMON HAVE AN OUTLINE?

Yes, the outline looked like this:

Introduction: It raises the question, "What's going on in this parable?" (paragraphs 1–10)

1. **We are tempted to get into a contract relationship with God.** (paragraphs 11–23)

Jesus didn't offer this parable as a model for settling wage disputes in the twenty-first century.

The parable is Jesus' response to two men who wanted to arrange a contract with God.

A wealthy young man approached Jesus with a question about the details of a business deal to get eternal life.

Peter and the other disciples asked another question that assumed a contract relationship with God for the service they rendered.

We often ask questions that imply that we are in a contract negotiation with God.

Jesus rejected the basic premise of those questions, which is that God enters into a contract with us.

Jesus responded to Peter's question with grace.

He could easily have made Peter feel guilty for bringing up the question of payment.

Jesus assured Peter that he and those like him would be fully paid for their service.

Then Jesus made the statement: BUT MANY WHO ARE FIRST WILL BE LAST, AND MANY WHO ARE LAST WILL BE FIRST (19:30). (This principle must be pivotal in our thinking. It tells us a basic lesson about how God deals with us)

2. **We will be rewarded not on the basis of our merit but on the basis of God's goodness and generosity.**
(Look at what this story shows us.) (paragraphs 24–35)

Service in the vineyard itself is a gift from God.

The workers standing idle in the marketplace just before sundown were not "the idle rich." They were the "idle poor."

Jesus comes to the idle, the unemployed, the lost and offers us meaningful work to do in His vineyard.

There is great fulfillment in serving the Lord in His vineyard.

Contract service—legalism—loses track of the fulfillment of having productive work to do.

(A second thing this story tells us is.)

God's goodness always determines His rewards.

The workers received unequal treatment, but it was never unjust treatment.

God in rewarding us always does so out of His great generosity.

Justice forms the background against which God's goodness appears as goodness and not unfairness.

When God deals with us, He doesn't want to give us wages; He wants to give us rewards.

(There is something else that comes clear to us in this story:)

We have no reason to want to strike a bargain in our dealings with God.

3. **Only a Self-Absorbed Person Grumbles against God's Goodness.** (paragraphs 36–41)

(How do you react to God's generosity and goodness?)

All of us appreciate God's goodness to us and respond with appreciation to it in our lives.

The question that tests me, however, is "How do I react to the goodness of God when it is shown to others?"

All of the workers were completely satisfied as long as they dealt with the vineyard owner alone.

Conclusion: Just as a father is honored by a son who works but doesn't work out a "contract," God is honored when we serve and leave the reward to Him. (paragraphs 42–43)

WHAT SHAPE DOES THIS SERMON TAKE?

It is an inductive-deductive sermon. The idea doesn't get stated until paragraph 22, which is well into the sermon. Once the idea is stated, it is briefly explained in paragraphs 23 and 24. Everything after that relates back to the idea and is deductive (as it always is when the idea is stated.)

WHAT TYPES OF SUPPORTING MATERIAL HAVE YOU USED IN THE SERMON?

There is a great deal of *restatement* throughout the sermon. It appears, for example, at the close of paragraphs 9, 10, 23, and 40 in the form of questions that form transitions from section to section. There is restatement that states again the idea of the previous section at the close of paragraph 30. All of paragraph 10 is basically restatement. That is true for paragraph 17 and 37 as well.

There is also *repetition* throughout the sermon. (Remember restatement states the same thing in different words, and repetition says the same thing in the same words.) There's a great deal of repetition in paragraphs 12–18 in order to focus on the question, "What's in it for me?"

There is *explanation* in the sermon. Paragraph 11, for instance, explains the importance of the context. Part of paragraph 24 is an explanation of "The first will be last and the last first." And paragraph 32 explains how all the workers in the parable were trusted with justice.

There is only one *quotation* in the sermon. It is the quote by Meister Eckhart found in paragraph 42. I used it because it was a helpful insight and not to quote an authority. Most people would have no idea who Eckhart was.

The sermon contains *narration*. The opening eight paragraphs narrate the parable with some modern touches. Dialogue is a special type of narration, and it is sprinkled throughout the message. It's in the conversation that Jesus had with Peter in paragraphs 19 and 20. It's in the questions and answer in paragraphs 37 and 38.

Three formal *illustrations* support the sermon. There is a brief illustration-quote from the Tartar tribes found in paragraph 30. (That is the only one that came from my files.) The other illustrations I used are personal. There is a brief illustration of a friend who lost his job in paragraph 26, and the sermon ends with a longer anecdote about my son in the final paragraph that I used to sum up the central idea.

WHAT ABOUT THE INTRODUCTION TO THE SERMON?

An effective introduction should accomplish three objectives. It gets attention, it surfaces a need, and it orients the audience to the body of the sermon. I tried to do that. (You can judge whether or not I was successful.)

The opening statement, "Jesus made a wise mid-career adjustment," was designed to get *attention*. Most people don't think of Jesus having a "career" or changing jobs.

I also tried to create *need* based on an appeal to curiosity. I tried to tell the parable so that listeners would ask, "What's that all about? The whole thing doesn't seem fair. Why would Jesus ever approve of an arrangement like that?" If it works, it is because the audience is saying to themselves, "He's got some explaining to do this morning!"

In spite of the old adage that "curiosity killed the cat and satisfaction brought it back again," I know that simply satisfying curiosity won't change lives. Later in the sermon, in paragraphs 13–16, I tried to surface a deeper, more personal need. Many people feel that God doesn't treat them fairly. That's the fundamental need this parable addresses, but I didn't know how to get at it directly. That's why I started with curiosity.

While I oriented people to the Scripture passage from the start, I oriented them to the body of the sermon in paragraphs 9 and 10 by raising the question, "Why did Jesus tell this story?" Because this sermon takes an inductive, rather than a deductive, development, I didn't orient listeners to the central idea or even to the subject of the sermon. Instead, I oriented them to the first movement in the message.

HOW ABOUT THE CONCLUSION? WHAT WERE YOU TRYING TO DO THERE?

A strong conclusion brings a sermon to "a burning focus" on the great idea of the sermon. The congregation should be brought back to the concept again and feel its weight and think of its implications. I attempted to do that in two ways. First, in paragraph 42 I summarized what I had been driving at throughout the sermon. I used the quote from Meister Eckhart to repeat the main idea in a fresh way. Then in the closing illustration about my son, I tried to get listeners to feel how God regards our positive response to his goodness.

To sum it up: Strong sermons should be bifocal. They must focus on the idea and the development of the text. Yet, they must also focus on the listener. Through bifocal preaching, those who hear come to understand and experience what the eternal God has to say to them today.

BIBLIOGRAPHY

Baumann, J. Daniel. *An Introduction to Contemporary Preaching.* Grand Rapids: Baker, 1972.

Beecher, Henry Ward. *Yale Lectures on Preaching.* New York: J. B. Ford, 1872.

Blackwood, Andrew W. *Expository Preaching for Today: Case Studies of Bible Passages.* Nashville: Abingdon-Cokesbury, 1953. Reprint, Grand Rapids: Baker, 1975.

Booth, John Nicholls. *The Quest for Preaching Power.* New York: Macmillan, 1943.

Brigance, William Norwood. *Speech: Its Techniques and Disciplines in a Free Society.* New York: Appleton-Century-Crofts, 1952.

Broadus, John A. *On the Preparation and Delivery of Sermons.* Rev. ed. Edited by Jesse Burton Weatherspoon. New York: Harper, 1944.

Brown, Charles R. *The Art of Preaching.* New York: Macmillan, 1922.

Bryant, Donald C., and Karl R. Wallace. *Fundamentals of Public Speaking.* New York: Appleton-Century, 1947. 3d ed. New York: Appleton-Century-Crofts, 1960.

Buechner, Frederick. *Telling the Truth.* New York: Harper and Row, 1977.

Buttrick, David. *Homiletic.* Philadelphia: Fortress, 1987.

Chapell, Bryan. *Christ-Centered Preaching.* Grand Rapids: Baker, 1994.

———. *Using Illustrations to Preach with Power.* Grand Rapids: Zondervan, 1992.

Cox, James W. *A Guide to Biblical Preaching.* Nashville: Abingdon, 1976.

Craddock, Fred B. *Preaching.* Nashville: Abingdon, 1985.

Davis, Flora. "How to Read Body Language." In *The Rhetoric of Nonverbal Communication: Readings,* edited by Haig A. Bosmajian. Glenview, Ill.: Scott, Foresman, 1971.

Davis, H. Grady. *Design for Preaching.* Philadelphia: Muhlenberg, 1958.

Dickens, Milton. *Speech: Dynamic Communication.* New York: Harcourt, Brace, 1954.

Duduit, Michael, ed. *Handbook of Contemporary Preaching.* Nashville: Broadman, 1992.

Eisenson, Jon, and Paul H. Boase. *Basic Speech.* 3d ed. New York: Macmillan, 1975.

Flesch, Rudolf. *The Art of Plain Talk.* New York: Harper, 1946.

Freeman, Harold. *Variety in Biblical Preaching.* Waco: Word, 1987.

Grasham, John A., and Glenn G. Gooder. *Improving Your Speech.* New York: Harcourt, Brace, 1960.

Gray, Giles W., and Claude M. Wise. *The Bases of Speech.* 3d ed. New York: Harper, 1959.

Hall, Edward T. *The Silent Language.* Garden City, N.Y.: Doubleday, 1959. Reprint, Greenwich, Conn.: Fawcett, 1968.

Haselden, Kyle. *The Urgency of Preaching.* New York: Harper and Row, 1963.

Hayakawa, S. I. *Language in Thought and Action.* 2d ed. New York: Harcourt, Brace and World, 1964.

Howe, Reuel L. *Partners in Preaching: Clergy and Laity in Dialogue.* New York: Seabury, 1967.

Jowett, J. H. *The Preacher: His Life and Work.* New York: George H. Doran, 1912. Reprint, Grand Rapids: Baker, 1968.

Larsen, David L. *Telling the Old, Old Story.* Wheaton: Crossway, 1995.

————. *The Anatomy of Preaching.* Grand Rapids: Baker, 1989.

Lewis, Ralph L., with Gregg Lewis. *Inductive Preaching.* Wheaton: Crossway, 1983.

Litfin, Duane. *Public Speaking.* 2d ed. Grand Rapids: Baker, 1992.

Lloyd-Jones, D. Martyn. *Preaching and Preachers.* Grand Rapids: Zondervan, 1971.

Logan, Samuel T., ed. *The Preacher and Preaching.* Phillipsburg, N.J.: Presbyterian and Reformed, 1986.

Long, Thomas G. *Preaching and the Literary Forms of the Bible.* Philadelphia: Fortress, 1989.

Macpherson, Ian. *The Art of Illustrating Sermons.* New York: Abingdon, 1964. Reprint, Grand Rapids: Baker, 1976.

Miller, Calvin. *Spirit, Word and Story.* Dallas: Word, 1989.

Miller, Donald G. *The Way to Biblical Preaching.* New York: Abingdon, 1957.

Minnick, Wayne C. *The Art of Persuasion.* Boston: Houghton Mifflin, 1957.

Monroe, Alan H. *Principles and Types of Speech.* 3d ed. Chicago: Scott, Foresman, 1949.

Monroe, Alan H., and Douglas Ehninger. *Principles and Types of Speech Communication.* 7th ed. Glenview, Ill.: Scott, Foresman, 1974.

Paget, Richard. *Human Speech: Some Observations, Experiments, and Conclusions as to the Nature, Origin, Purpose, and Possible Improvement of Human Speech.* New York: Harcourt, Brace, 1930.

Pelsma, John R. *Essentials of Speech.* Rev. ed. New York: Crowell, 1924.

Pitt-Watson, Ian. *A Primer for Preachers.* Grand Rapids: Baker, 1986.

Reid, Loren D. *Speaking Well.* Columbia, Mo.: Artcraft, 1962.

Reu, J. M. *Homiletics: A Manual of the Theory and Practice of Preaching.* Translated by Albert Steinhaeuser. Chicago: Wartburg, 1924. Reprint, Grand Rapids: Baker, 1967.

Robinson, Haddon W. *Biblical Sermons.* Grand Rapids: Baker, 1989.

————. *Making a Difference in Preaching.* Grand Rapids: Baker, 1999.

Sangster, William E. *The Craft of Sermon Construction.* Philadelphia: Westminster, 1951. Reprint, Grand Rapids: Baker, 1972.

Sarett, Alma Johnson, Lew Sarett, and William Trufant Foster. *Basic Principles of Speech.* 4th ed. Boston: Houghton Mifflin, 1966.

Schultze, Quentin. *Communicating for Life.* Grand Rapids: Baker, 2000.

Soper, Donald O. *The Advocacy of the Gospel.* New York: Abingdon, 1961.

Stibbs, Alan M. *Expounding God's Word: Some Principles and Methods.* Grand Rapids: Eerdmans, 1961.

Stott, John. *Between Two Worlds.* Grand Rapids: Eerdmans, 1982.

Sunukjian, Donald R. "Patterns for Preaching: A Rhetorical Analysis of the Sermons of Paul in Acts 13, 17, and 20." Th.D. diss., Dallas Theological Seminary, 1972.

Thielicke, Helmut. *Encounter with Spurgeon.* Translated by John W. Doberstein. Philadelphia: Fortress, 1963. Reprint, Grand Rapids: Baker, 1975.

Thompson, Wayne N. *Quantitative Research in Public Address and Communication.* New York: Random, 1967.

Thonssen, Lester, and A. Craig Baird. *Speech Criticism: The Development of Standards for Rhetorical Appraisal.* New York: Ronald, 1948.

Tizard, Leslie J. *Preaching: The Art of Communication.* London: Allen and Unwin, 1958.

Whitesell, Faris D., and Lloyd M. Perry. *Variety in Your Preaching.* Old Tappan, N.J.: Revell, 1954.

Whitesell, Faris D., ed. *Great Expository Sermons.* Westwood, N.J.: Revell, 1964.

Wiersbe, Warren W. *Preaching and Teaching with Imagination.* Wheaton: Victor, 1994.

Willhite, Keith, and Scott Gibson, eds. *The Big Idea of Biblical Preaching.* Grand Rapids: Baker, 1998.

Williams, George G. *Creative Writing for Advanced College Classes.* Rev. ed. New York: Harper, 1954.

Willimon, William H., and Richard Lischer, eds. *Concise Encyclopedia of Preaching.* Louisville: Westminster/John Knox, 1995.

Wilson, Paul Scott. *The Four Pages of the Sermon: A Complete Guide to Biblical Preaching.* Nashville: Abingdon, 2000.

———. *The Practice of Preaching.* Nashville: Abingdon, 1995.

Wood, John. *The Preacher's Workshop: Preparation for Expository Preaching.* Chicago: InterVarsity, 1965.

INDEX OF PERSONS

INDEX OF SCRIPTURE